ESTHER'S NOTEBOOKS

Riad Sattouf
ESTHER'S NOTEBOOKS

Translated from the French by Sam Taylor

PANTHEON BOOKS
NEW YORK

All rights reserved. Published in the United States by Pantheon Books, a division of Penguin Random House LLC, New York, and distributed in Canada by Penguin Random House Canada Limited, Toronto. Originally published in France in three volumes as *Les cahiers d'Esther* by Allary Éditions, Paris, in 2016 and 2017. Copyright © Allary Éditions and Riad Sattouf. This translation originally published in hardcover in Great Britain as three volumes entitled *Esther's Notebooks* by Pushkin Press, London, in 2021.

Pantheon Books and colophon are registered trademarks of Penguin Random House LLC.

Library of Congress Cataloging-in-Publication Data
Names: Sattouf, Riad, author, artist. | Taylor, Sam, [date] translator.
Title: Esther's notebooks / Riad Sattouf ; translated from the French by Sam Taylor.
Other titles: Cahiers d'Esther. English
Description: First American edition. | New York : Pantheon Books, 2022
Identifiers: LCCN 2022008175 (print). LCCN 2022008176 (ebook). ISBN 9780593316924 (hardcover). ISBN 9780593316931 (ebook).
Subjects: LCSH: Children—France—Paris—Comic books, strips, etc. Manners and customs—Comic books, strips, etc. Paris (France)—Social life and customs—Comic books, strips, etc. | LCGFT: Biographical comics. Humorous comics. Graphic novels.
Classification: LCC PN6747.S247 C3413 2022 (print) | LCC PN6747.S247 (ebook) | DDC 741.5/6944—dc23/eng/20220331
LC record available at https://lccn.loc.gov/2022008175
LC ebook record available at https://lccn.loc.gov/2022008176

www.pantheonbooks.com

Thanks to Matthieu Croissandeau

This book is supported by the Institut Français (Royaume-Uni) as part of the Burgess programme.

Jacket illustration by Riad Sattouf
Jacket design by Chip Kidd
Book design by Tetragon and Lucie Cohen

Printed in China
First American Edition
2 4 6 8 9 7 5 3 1

Part 1
Tales from My 10-Year-Old Life

The Family

My name is Esther and I'm 9 years old. I live in Paris, in the 17th arrondissement.

My dad is a sports trainer or something in this place where people go to do sport. My mum works in a bank.

They've been together a long time. There's a photo of them when they were young on the fridge.

I have a big brother called Antoine. We share the same bedroom. He gave me some headphones so I wouldn't bother him. He doesn't like any of my music.

I'm in Year 5 at a private school. My dad says it's better for me at my age.

My brother goes to a normal school that my parents don't pay for. In the morning he feels sick and doesn't want to go. He's not a very good student.

My best friend at school is Eugenie. I like Cassandra too. Actually I get on pretty well with everybody.

At school, we can talk to each other how we want. It's not like being at home, where you're not allowed to swear.

But I don't like to swear much. It's trashy, not classy. Boys are trashy, for example. They swear all the time when they're doing two things: playing football and talking to girls. But anyway, who cares about boys?

Eugenie is really lucky because she's rich. She already has the iPhone 6! And at home she's got an iPad and a computer and she even has a TV in her bedroom.

If I could just have an iPhone – even a 4 – I'd be so happy. But I'm poor.

I'm even the poorest one in my family.

(Based on a true story told by Esther, who is 9 years old)

Riad Sattouf

7

Mums and Dads

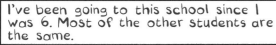

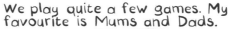

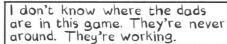
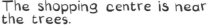

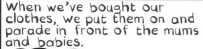

(Based on a true story told by Esther, who is 9 years old)

Riad Sattouf

Antoine

My brother Antoine and I sleep in the same room. He's 14 and he's a bit stupid, but that's normal for a boy.

This is me reading "Stars Like", a very interesting magazine about stars

♪ YO, HOMIE ♪

At ten o'clock, my dad comes to switch off the light. But Antoine keeps listening to his trashy music in bed.

The singer's name is La Fouine (that means The Weasel)

Get your gun and shoot him in the head WE DON'T GIVE A FUCK! Can't buy it in stores we sell in bulk instead WE DON'T GIVE A FUCK!

→ He whispers the lyrics

I'm in my Porsche, eating a kebab WE DON'T GIVE A FUCK! Talk shit about me, better watch yo' back COS WE DON'T GIVE A FUCK!

He looks really annoyed

So I stick my fingers in my ears and imagine someone's given me a KidiSecrets.

It's an electronic diary for keeping your secrets safe!

The screen is heart-shaped — cool.

FOR ME?

My dad hates them

Esther! Pssst! Esther! Hey!

Can you tell me about your day, with loads of details? That way, I might be able to fall asleep...

HUH? OH PFFT!

I'LL DO THE SAME FOR YOU!

Pleeeaaase

PFFT... All right then, I got up and I went to the kitchen for

NO, more details! How many steps did you take? Tell me everything.

Okay, let's see... One step to put my first foot out of bed, and another to stand up... After that, one step to put on my left slipper, no, I mean my right, but... well, sometimes it's the left...

That's it...

And then, one step, two steps, hang on... one, two, three... four steps to the door...

Mmm

He always falls asleep before I drink my hot chocolate.

Zzzzz

Psst! Antoine! Are you asleep? It's your turn to tell me about your day!

AN-TOINE!

... I got up and I went to my shitty school and then I went to bed and that's it...

Zzzzz

(Based on a true story told by Esther, who is 9 years old)

Riad Sattouf

Kidnapper Alert

I have a great social life. My friends really love me.

This is me in the playground, listening to my friend Eugenie who's telling me about a photograph

It's break time

?!?

.. and my cousin's laughing and he shows me his phone and I see a photo of TAL with a boy "doing things" on the beach! I WAS SHOCKED, YO!

I don't know what to say about boys except that we don't talk about them because they're, you know, boys.

What things?

Y'know, kissing and stuff

The boys are playing over there

The girls are here →

Boys are nasty. They're supposed to be nasty. It's normal, that's just how they are. But sometimes they go too far.

ZLATAN! ZLATAN!

YEAH FUCKING ZLATAN

They shout that when they score a goal

For example, the other day, me, Eugenie, Cassandra and Violet were playing something, I can't remember what...

Oh, you're so beautiful

Hee hee

My name is Rapunzel, what's yours?

... when suddenly boys started running from all directions to kidnap us.

They were being quiet and looked really mean

A kidnapping is when lots of boys get together and decide to take a girl to one of their friends. They force her and it's bad but it doesn't happen very often.

KIDNAPPER ALERT

KIDNAPPER ALERT!

At first, I thought they were going to kidnap me (I've been kidnapped loads before and that day I was wearing my red dress and velvet boots) but actually they came for Violet.

Mpf! Mpf!

They took her to the boy who'd ordered the kidnapping (it was Maxime, a big show-off who all the girls hate) and she started crying. She knew she would never see her parents again.

You're mine till you die.

WAAAAH

Us girls tried to save her but the other boys hit us. So we went to fetch the teacher, Miss Morret (the ugly one).

Miss! Violet's been kidnapped! It's bad, yo!

?

She's always looking at her phone even though we're not allowed to

---

The teacher went over and yelled at the boys. Maxime managed not to cry.

WHAT'S THE BIG DEAL?

Violet started shouting too then and she told the teacher to leave Maxime alone because she belonged to him now.

GET YOUR HANDS OFF MY HUSBAND!

In the end, everybody cried. So that's what boys are like. Bad.

And I really thought Violet was too ugly to ever be kidnapped!

WAAAAH

WAAAAH

(Based on a true story told by Esther, who is 9 years old)

Riad Sattouf

The Popular Singer

Me and my brother don't talk much, but we watch TV together.

On Saturday, we were alone in the house because our parents were out shopping

My brother had the remote and we were watching NRJ "Hit Music Only," a really cool TV program that shows music videos.

Helloooo yoohoo!

Yesss this song rocks!

This track is dedicated to Mrs Pavoshko! You remember? Mr Diallo!

You know this one, right?

Yeah!

The singer is called Black M and I think he's one of the most popular singers in France. But it's mostly boys who like him.

Hey, Mrs Pavoshko, yo
I'm not in prison or a mental hospital, no
I'm a star, Mrs Pavoshko
And your kids dig me, Mrs Pavoshko

In this song, he's talking about a school headmistress who didn't believe in him, so he takes his revenge in the song.

Yo, you remember me, the little black kid who wrote crazy verses like Fuck the Teacher? Pass me the mic!

FUCK THE TEACHER

I was hoping I could watch "Tangled" again

I like that song, it's catchy and Black M is very handsome (that's also why he's very popular).

I don't give a BEEP yeah
Yeah, I know, it's a shame
I'm being censored
and you're to blame
YEAH YEAH YEAH!

My brother knew all the words to the song. He's good at learning, so I don't know why he's so bad at school.

All alone, head underwater, I thought it's time to start a fire!

START A FIRE!

But my parents came home and my dad recognized the song straight away.

TURN THAT RUBBISH OFF NOW!

HUH? YOU SERIOUS, YO?

All alone, head underwater, I thought...

THAT TUNE IS A DISEASE! YOU CATCH IT WITHOUT EVEN NOTICING AND IT STAYS IN YOUR HEAD FOR DAYS! TURN IT OFF NOW, I DON'T WANT TO HEAR IT!

I'M LISTENING TO THIS!

It's time to start a fire...

My dad teaches sport so he's much stronger than Antoine. So he changed the channel.

Come on, an advertising jingle, anything...

And this is REALLY good news...

Mrs Pavoshko was right when she said that guy would be a waste of space! That song is rubbish!

How can anyone like that crap?

Yeah, like you've got really good taste in music!

Dad put on a programme he likes on RMC Discovery. It's about men driving very fast cars. But it was too late: the tune was stuck in his head.

All alone, head underwater, I thought it's time to start a fire
GRRRRR!

I didn't dare ask if I could watch "Tangled"

Oh my word, that's five seconds faster than Harry

(Based on a true story told by Esther, who is 9 years old)

Riad Sattouf

11

Maxime

A private school is a school you have to pay for. I don't really know why my dad chose this school, because we're not rich.

I'll explain why later. It's better for girls your age. You don't get so many little punks in private schools.

My dad is very stylish

I love him

I think he's scared that the boys will hurt me. He's right — boys are horrible. In my class, for example, Maxime is super-nasty.

Hello bitch!

Sometimes he would spit at us for no reason.

WHAT'S WRONG WITH YOU?

YO, IT'S ALL OVER YOU

Actually he mostly spat at Cassandra

Ha ha

He did impressions of us in class in front of everyone. The girls really hated him.

Miiisss, can I go to the toilets?

Miiisss, can I go poo-poo?

HA HA HA HA HA

And then, the other day, he got out of his dad's car and he wasn't dressed the same way any more.

CLACK!

His dad is very very rich

He came into the playground and started swaggering around like a cool dude, listening to music on headphones.

Everybody fell silent. All the girls stared at him.

Huh, what's he doing?

He's got Blueteeth headphones, did you see?

But, that's against the...

I went to talk to Maxime because nobody else dared.

HEY! YOU'RE NOT ALLOWED TO WEAR HEADPHONES IN THE PLAYGROUND, I'M GOING TO TELL THE TEACHER!

HAHA SHUT UP... YOU THINK I'M SCARED?

I'VE GOT THE SAME JACKET AS MAÎTRE GIMS, BITCH.

Maître Gims is the most famous person in France. He's a singer that everybody likes. He's the most popular boy ever.

You never see his eyes

This is him at the start of the video for "Changer", a really cool song

Lenco

He's very rich: he shows off his tablet in the video

I didn't even need to tell the teacher. She confiscated his headphones and his baseball cap.

Seriously, yo, it's too much, showing off like that!

Cassandra, what's the matter?

Waaah!

He... sniff... he's too good-looking... like a star... and... and... he hates me!

Waaah!

Maxime always spat at Cassandra. But, just like all the other girls at school, she'd fallen in love with him.

(Based on a true story told by Esther, who is 9 years old)

Riad Sattouf

Mitchell

My dad says boys in private schools aren't as crazy as ones in schools you don't have to pay for (yes, my dad thinks boys are crazy, and he's right).

This is me in my favourite dress blowing in the wind

The worst boy in my class, the one all the girls really hate, is Mitchell.

Don't you want to play with me?

SHUT YOUR MOUTH

I don't like swear words but I say them to him

He wants to play with girls!!!

The other boys hate him because they're nasty, but we hate him because he doesn't understand anything about life.

Just one time! At the game you like!

GO AWAY! STOP FOLLOWING US!!!

WE TOLD YOU: NEVER!

He's English or something

He's really poor, for a start. He doesn't like gadgets, he doesn't have a phone, and he kisses his dad in front of everybody.

Have a good day, my boy

Speaking English

MWAH

Plus he's extremely ugly and his body is weird. He runs with his back straight, like a robot.

Eugenie's really good at copying him

HU! HU! HU!

EVERYBODY GET IN LINE

This is us in PE

But the worst thing is that he keeps on being nice even though everybody hates him.

PASS THE FUCKING BALL!

FUCK

Even the boys pretend he doesn't exist

But he still runs around with them like everything is normal

The other day, he did something terrible.

VIOLET, I... I LOVE YOU...

?

HUH

GASP

HUH

Violet was shocked, so she and her friends grabbed Mitchell and beat him up.

They hurt him really badly. And then the teacher saw them.

Waaah!

Violet and her friends were punished, and Mitchell went to a corner and cried and cried.

WAAAAH!

WAAAH!

Anyway, despite that, the other day, he did something else really bad. It was the end of term, so the teacher gave us all Kinder eggs.

KINDER EGGS, MY FAVOURITE THING IN THE WHOLE WORLD!

who hasn't had their

Okay then, you can have mine, Esther!

I hesitated, but it was a Kinder, the best thing in the world, so I took it.

Thanks

GASP

WHAAT

OMG

HUH

HA HA HA!

SHE LOVES HIM

HA HA

SHHH, THAT'S ENOUGH

HA HA

HAHA

HA

Esther loves Mitchell

Mitchell really is the worst boy in the world.

(Based on a true story told by Esther, who is 9 years old)

Riad Sattouf

Bendy Bodies

I want to be a singer when I'm older. A famous singer, like TAL, for example (she's got dark hair and the voice of an angel).

You say "I love you" every where

This is me at my dance class, where we're doing a routine to "International" by TAL

HF HF

Everywheere

But you take me I don't know where, you say "I love you" everywheeere

---

I've noticed something. Popular, famous people are very good-looking, but they also have something else in common: bendy bodies.

You send my heart internationaaaal

Hmpf Inter Hmpf National

The other leg Esther

Youu send my heart internationaaaal

Tal, for example, she's a really good mover. Dynamic.

I love this hip-hop part in her song "International"

Hey yo one two one time for your mind zis is how we do iiiit

Really good

Yannick Noah is very good-looking (and very famous), and I heard he used to be a sports teacher, like Dad.

We run, we live, we run, we die, we say stop, it's over

The video for "On Court" is amazing

My dad is very very good-looking. And he can do the splits too.

Hmpf! You have to stretch

Ha ha careful you don't squash your...

OH!

Hee hee

See?

Hmpf

My brother

Papa can also stand on his hands and bend over backwards.

Seriously, that's gross, just stop...

Hee hee

My brother is so ugly that I don't even want to talk about it

Hmpf

The president of France... what's his name again? Oh yes, François Hollande. Anyway, he's good-looking, of course, because you can't be president if you're ugly. But I don't know how bendy he is (I suppose he must be).

My dad doesn't want me to watch the news, he says it's too shocking

Ah, no, Hollande! Don't watch this!

Actually he doesn't like anybody on TV

It's normal that celebrities are good-looking. People are inspired when they see people who are better-looking than them.

For example, I'd like to have hair in front of my eyes like Shakira so I'd look all mysterious

But my mum wants me to have a fringe so I can see what I'm writing

---

For example, our teacher Miss Morret is really really ugly. Nobody's inspired by her.

When she bends over, I feel like I'm going to throw up

13,25 +14

OOOF

Or the woman who lives in the office near the front door of our apartment building.

Every time, she looks at me like she's never seen me before

Or my mum, for example... She was very beautiful when she was young. Nowadays, she's not as bendy as she used to be.

I - CAN'T - DO - IT - ANY - MORE

Not that she really tries very hard.

Esther, go and get me a glass of water. My back's killing me.

I adore her

Thankfully, I take more after my dad.

Yo, doesn't it hurt when you do that?

It's like she's got detachable legs!

Hmpf!

I'm good-looking. (It's not me who says that, it's the others)

(Based on a true story told by Esther, who is 9 years old)

Riad Sattouf

Gay People

My school is a primary school, for kids aged 6 to 11.

This is me arriving in the playground with some of the younger kids (I don't talk to them)

A funny thing happened this week. A boy from Year 2 walked past carrying his schoolbag and it touched Abdou's bottom.

Abdou is a big boy from Year 6 who's tall enough to be in secondary school. His dad works in politics or something.

OI! DON'T TOUCH MY ARSE, YOU QUEER!

QUEER!

? ?! ??

Hey Abdou, what's "QUEER"?

Gays, you know? They're gross...

Really nice guy

I know what gay people are: two men who love each other (two bald men, usually). Sometimes they can be women, but that's rare.

URGH ESTHER YOU'RE QUEER, YO

HA HA

After that, everybody in the playground started calling each other queer. It was really funny.

HAHA gotcha Esther!

DON'T TOUCH ME, YOU QUEER!

You're a QUEER

She's QUEER

HA

The next day, that little Year 2 kid pointed at Abdou, who was wearing a blue watch and an orange jacket.

Blue and orange are the colours of queers!

?

WAK!

Afterwards, Abdou was so angry that he told a monitor about the Year 2 kid.

And then he said I was queer, sir, he can't say that

Why did he say that?

I'm not queer, sir

He never notices anything

I don't think there are any gay kids in my school. Oh, wait, I did see two Year 6 boys kissing and rolling on the ground in front of everybody.

I was shocked

I don't see the point in being gay. You can't have children. Violet told me that she and her parents had gone on a protest march to stop gay people adopting.

We chanted "A mum and a dad, every child deserves that"!

It was great!

It must be horrible having two Dads! Can you imagine? They'd never be home because they were too busy working, and they wouldn't be able to cook or keep the house clean...

Aren't you hungry?

I'm really hungry

You go! You go!

HA HA

But when you think about it, it's weird that people think being gay is a bad thing. I don't really know what that's about.

And Mum's not even home yet...

And it takes her so long to get dinner ready...

Yeah HAHA

(Based on a true story told by Esther, who is 9 years old)

Riad Sattouf

The Mystery of Father Christmas

I really like going in shops, especially when it's Christmas (I like the decorations).

This is my family at a giant shopping centre called Vélizy 2

Before I stopped believing in Father Christmas, I saw so many strange things.

For a start, when we went to Auchan, just before Christmas, there were always more toys than usual. And the people around us all had carts full of toys.

Why are they buying them when Father Christmas will bring them for free?

The weird thing is that my dad told me magic and God didn't exist, but Father Christmas did.

Hey Antoine, Father Christmas doesn't exist, does he?

Well I don't give a...

Antoine

Answer your little sister! Go on, sweetheart!

Um, oh... Well, yeah, he does exist... um...

Nooo! Seriously, you still believe? At your age?

My dad told me that God, Jesus and magic were all invented by intelligent people to manipulate less intelligent people without them realizing.

Hey, you shouldn't threaten your son like that, wallah

"Wallah"? That's new!

But it's obvious that God and Jesus don't exist: you only ever see paintings of them, never photographs.

Ha ha what rubbish!

Shhh, sweet-heart.

This is us visiting a church in La Rochelle last summer

Mathilde, in my class, told me she met Jesus in a church once.

He smiled at me. I sat on his lap and touched his beard!

Hee hee

REALLY?

When I visited the church in La Rochelle, I also saw someone who looked like Jesus, but it was just a man who was homeless.

Anyway, after a while, my dad finally admitted that everybody gave each other presents at Christmas, and it had nothing to do with Father Christmas.

I knew it!

So last year, I knew who'd given me each present (Mum and Dad: the flying fairy; Granny: nature cards)... until I found an incredible present that I hadn't asked for but I'd really wanted!

My granny

THE GLACIATION PLASMA POKÉMON! WHO GAVE ME THIS?

Huh? Was it you? No

Um, not me

GASP!

Incredible but true: nobody had given me that present! But there it was! Since then, I've started believing in Father Christmas again.

(Based on a true story told by Esther, who is 9 years old)

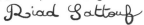

Riad Sattouf

The Truth About Father Christmas

This year, we went to my granny's house for Christmas, like we do almost every year.

This is me in a street in Bain-de-Bretagne, the place where she lives.

She lives in a small house, and in the house next door I have a friend I see every year because she visits her grandparents at Christmas too.

Eugenie!!!

Hi there!

Her name is Eugenie too, like my friend in Paris! Weird, huh?

We're allowed to go on the path behind our houses. So on the day before Christmas, we went for a walk.

Listen to this, it's the NRJ MUSIC AWARDS 2014 compilation... "Andalouse" by Kendji Girac... I got it for Christmas...

WHAT? BUT CHRISTMAS IS TOMORROW! HOW DID...

Yeah, but we gave each other presents yesterday because my dad has to go back to work today...

Ebony eyes, I like to see you move like a queen, your body glides...

Kendji Girac is a famous singer and a Gitano (I don't know what that means)

And there it was: the proof that Father Christmas didn't actually exist.

I was about to start crying when suddenly...

GASP!

BRR!

It came towards us. It was so SO beautiful! It looked at us.

BRHH

It smelled of horse

You could see its muscles!

! !

In a flash, I no longer cared that Father Christmas didn't exist! I was crazy about that horse.

My friend ran away

AGHH

But she loved it too

Afterwards, me and Eugenie went to her house and started a horse lovers' club that we called "Horse Stars". It's for sharing information among people who are interested in horses.

We googled all the possible horse colours and wrote them down on a sheet of paper, in case anyone was interested

– Cremello
– perlino
– palomino...

And then, on Christmas Eve...

So what do you think Father Christmas's secret present will be this year, sweetheart?

Granny

Dad

My brother Antoine

Mum

BLAH BLAH BLAH I KNOW THE TRUTH SO STOP TELLING ME RUBBISH. I KNOW FATHER CHRISTMAS DOESN'T EXIST.

But I would like you to buy me a horse next Christmas.

Everybody was shocked, but at least things were clear now.

What the...

Just to be clear, before everybody blames me, I didn't tell her.

(Based on a true story told by Esther, who is 9 years old)

Riad Sattouf

The Charlie

This week, something really bad happened. My best friend Eugenie called me "really annoying".

Sorry but you're not my best friend any more, yo

Cassandra watched us

Give me back your BFF necklace

This is me, in shock

The BFF necklace is a heart that breaks in two and each best friend wears half of it.

Cassandra told Eugenie "Yeah, Esther doesn't get why you tell me things but you don't tell her", and that's when Eugenie said "She's really annoying sometimes"

Thank you

You're welcome

It really hurt my feelings. Oh, and I also know that some terrorists attacked the Charlie (which is either a person or a newspaper, I'm not too sure) because the Charlie made fun of their God.

Go to your bedroom, sweetheart.

This horrifying event took place

Then at school everybody was talking about it and there was a man who came to the playground to give a speech, but I didn't really understand what he was talking about.

He was talking "politics". It was really annoying

Our teacher Miss Morret yes, she's a woman even though she doesn't look like one

It was about the Charlie

Talking "politics" means, um, I don't know, it's... For example, he said in this really deep, strange voice, "Fraternity... Equality..." and the other word that goes with them, I can't remember what it is. What's the other word?

Something very serious happened, but I can't tell you what. We're all going to have a minute's silence later.

I swear, that's what he said

He was wearing president's clothes – all grey with those fake shoulders that make them look super-straight. He talked and talked and then, after a while, he shouted "And now close your eyes and SILENCE!"

When he said that, everybody closed their eyes, but it woke me up

I tried to hold it in, but I couldn't. I started laughing. Their faces just looked really really funny.

HEE HEE

But seriously, you should have seen Mitchell!

The man in president's clothes and the teacher both gave me a nasty look.

Hee hee

I closed my eyes

After that, we went to class and the teacher told us about the different religions by showing us their signs. The cross of death for the Christians, the crescent for the Muslims and the star for the Jews.

Here!

Ahh

Kalila raised her hand and said that she was a Muslim and she'd never heard of the "crescent" sign. The teacher said, "Oh really?"

But there are crescents on mosques sometimes...

I didn't know that Kalila was Muslim. She said she didn't agree with the terrorists but that the Charlie shouldn't have made fun of their God. I agree: I think it's better not to make fun of gods, actually.

She knew all about it! But then she is very rich – she has an iPhone 6 Plus and she can go on the internet...

That's all I'm saying!

Then some girls started crying. One of them was Eugenie.

Waaah

Waaaaaaah

I went over to give her a hug.

I'm scared that the terrorists will come to our school and kill us

No, it's okay, they went home, it's all over now

Waaaaaaaah

And that's when she said that I wasn't annoying at all and she gave me a BFF bracelet (she'd given the necklace to another girl) so I would forgive her!

So at least it had a happy ending!

(Based on a true story told by Esther, who is 9 years old)

Riad Sattouf

18

The Wedding

(Based on a true story told by Esther, who is 9 years old)

Turning 10

This week, I turned 10 years old.

This is me and my family celebrating my birthday at Pizza Pino because their four-cheese pizza is my favourite meal in the whole world

I got a flower-patterned jacket as a present.

Exactly what I wanted

BYOO-TI-FUL

The next day, I put it on and went to school.

Yo, what's good is that it's your own style, I mean it wouldn't suit me, for example...

My friend Eugenie

I went to see Louis, my husband (we got married last week, remember). He was with his friends.

Hello, lover.

Whoa, pink flowers, fuck me!

?

He didn't come to my birthday party.

Louis will be here soon, he

You think? I got a text from Violet saying he's been with Elodie all day...

Oh yeah I knew that course I did um

This is me trying hard not to cry

In fact, he got a divorce without telling me. Now he has another wife.

Please don't tell my mum what I did with it

One of the people who hang out in front of the Franprix took the coat and good luck to them.

(Based on a true story told by Esther, who is 10 years old)

Riad Sattouf

The Curse

This week, my best friend Eugenie invited me to her country house in Fontainebleau.

This is me in my Peruvian hat and my dad driving me there

He complains all the time and I love it →

For God's sake, look at these mansions! It's outrageous

Eugenie's parents are rich. They have a house in Paris, a house in Fontainebleau, a house by the sea, a house in the mountains, and another one somewhere else.

If I were president, I'd confiscate all their houses

Don't worry, Esther is in good hands!

See you Sunday. Better go inside before you catch cold!

SWEE-TIE!

COOL, YO!

Slow down, Eugenie. You might fall!

LEAVE ME ALONE!

KR KR

I've never seen her dad

Eugenie hates her mum, it's weird

I don't know why because she's really nice. It's amazing how big her breasts are though. Each one is bigger than her head.

Manners, Eugenie!

Scarily big

She dresses in really tight clothes so you can always see the shape of her body, whatever she's doing.

And don't leave your shoes on the floor!

She wears jodhpurs even though she doesn't have a horse!

We spent the afternoon in the house. We're not allowed to go in the garden because it's too big. We were getting bored but then Eugenie had an idea.

WHY DON'T WE LOOK IN MY SISTERS' BEDROOMS AND SEE WHAT WE CAN FIND?

SURE, YEAH!

Eugenie has two sisters. The oldest is 19.

So? Any love letters? She's got a boyfriend, and when he comes here they close the door and make these weird noises

No, I can't see anything...

We didn't find anything but then I opened the wardrobe and found a pair of knickers with a string.

STRANGE!

You think the string goes in front?

In the second bedroom, we found a bra. A bra is two bags where women can keep their breasts if they want to.

GASP

We looked at it and I laughed because I'd never seen such a huge bra before.

YUCK!

We could almost sit inside each breast-bag.

Eugenie do you want to come under the big tent?

HA HA

AHEUUUUUHHH

That evening, her sisters arrived and I realized why Eugenie hated her mum. She's scared that one day it will happen to her.

HI GIRLS!

Hello!

(Based on a true story told by Esther, who is 10 years old)

Riad Sattouf

21

The Fly

It's really annoying having to share my bedroom. But we have no choice because we're not very rich.

This is me listening to Voltage FM.

My brother Antoine is so horrible, he enjoys watching others suffer (but it's normal because he's a boy).

This is him. I hate him

Estheeer!

A FLYyyyyy

Bzzzz

I know this is weird, but the things that scare me most in the world are flies.

Honestly, this drawing terrifies me

I can't even look at it

Even just talking about them, I feel like I'm about to cry.

THE FLY IS HEEERE

People say they're not, but I feel sure that flies are intelligent.

Hey, it's landed on you!

Boys are disgusting

They fly right at me and I'm sure they're trying to get in my nostrils or my ears or my mouth.

AARRGGHH

THE FLY! THE FLY IS HERE!

My dad, the hero

QUE PASA?

AARRGGHH

THE FLY! THE FLY

SHUT IT!

My dad is an angel.

I've never met anyone like him.

CLAK

I find it really hard to believe he's a boy.

(Based on a true story told by Esther, who is 10 years old)

Riad Sattouf

22

The Popular Boys

I've always gone to this private school. I've never been anywhere else.

This is me walking into the playground

In my school, you're not allowed to wear a baseball cap or have footballer hair

My dad says that in free schools, the boys are violent to girls, and they're wild.

My brother →

ESTHER I'M GOING TO KIIIIILLL YOU

HHH

AGH!

I think he's right, because my brother Antoine is in a free school and he's totally weird.

HA HA HA

NAH I'M NOT REALLY GOING TO KILL YOU, SIS

HA HA

The other day, he came home from school and he kept asking my mum if we were originally from another country.

Nope, we're just from Paris

Even if you go back a long way? Y'know, grannies and all that

No, sorry

So there aren't any Rebeus in our family?

Or any Renois?

No? Hmm...

MUUUUUUUUM?

WHAT ARE REBEUS AND RENOIS?

So he explained to us that Rebeus means Arab and Renois means Black, and how all the popular boys in his school have foreign origins...

Stefan, representing Romania

Always in my heart

I'm Enzo the Italiano, whassup yo

Amar, Senegal 1 France 0 for life yo

Hey, this is Amine the Tunisiano.

Reprezent!

They all have footballer hair →

The others are just boring Babtous (which means whites).

My name is Gaspard, I'm from Paris

I'm Thomas

...

No footballer hair because Dad said no

So all the Babtous tried to find foreign origins, however distant.

Yo, I'm Gaspard and I represent Portugal...

Don't try anything

Toto from España!

...

(His uncle's wife is Portuguese)

(Half-Spanish great-grandfather)

My dad never agrees with Antoine, so he started yelling at him.

Who cares about origins? That's nationalism, being proud of your origins! All the world's problems are caused by nationalism!

Rise above it!

Come on, Dad, please, just let me get a Jérémy Ménez haircut! Pleeease!

NO

Jérémy Ménez AC Milan

Hey, wait, Granny's from Brittany! You just have to call yourself "Antoine the Bretonno"

Smart girl!

Well yeah!

(Based on a true story told by Esther, who is 10 years old)

Riad Sattouf

23

The Baby Cat

Some of my friends went skiing in the February holidays. We went to my grandmother's house in Bain-de-Bretagne.

My dad → My mum → My brother | The rain → | My granny → | And me

In my opinion, God probably doesn't exist, because he never granted the two wishes I made to him.

Oh Lord let me be blonde and please let me have an iPhone

Your humble servant, Esther

For the 14,259th time, no iPhone before secondary school.

Go play with Eugenie.

Booooring

Pardon?

When I go to my grandmother's house, I play with my friend Eugenie (the other Eugenie, I mean, not the one from Paris). I see her every time I come here because she visits her granny during the holidays too.

Look, it's a game where you look after a cat

WHOA TOO COOL

She has an iPad all to herself

It's only the best game in the whole wide world! It's called "My Angela" or something like that.

If you stroke it, the baby cat purrs

prrrrr prrrr

The bathroom is pink — beautiful

The idea is that you have to look after the baby cat and it's just like a real baby: in the game, it grows up and turns into a teenage cat and then a woman cat.

CLAK   CLAK

You can even hit it and then it falls over, it's super-realistic

Ah Ah

You have to feed it, brush its teeth, give it baths and put it to bed, and like that you win gold coins.

Mmm! Glub glub!

CLING CLING

And then, with the gold coins, you can buy dresses or hairstyles, but they're really expensive.

A few examples:

Afro hair (1,680 coins)   Long blonde hair (25 diamonds)   Hipster hat (1,080 coins)

Tiara (75 diamonds)   Hair shaved on one side (free)   Floppy hat (3,000 coins)

And if you want more, you have to buy diamonds.

I'm going to buy 4,000, that's 99 euros... That way, we can buy everything. I know my dad's password — it's my name.

4,000 diamonds = 440,000 coins

Since we were very rich, we bought everything, even the food. But the cat didn't want to eat so Eugenie hit it — it was horrible.

EAT, DAMN YOU! COME ON, EAT!

CLAK CLAK CLAK CLAK CLAK CLAK

It made me cry

She was crazy

After a few days, Eugenie's dad came into our room and he slapped his daughter.

They'd emailed him the 99 euros receipt

CLAK

He took away her iPad for ever.

You can go home, Esther. Eugenie is grounded for the rest of the holiday.

Waaaah

MIAOWW mummy I'm hungry... mummy where are you?

(Based on a true story told by Esther, who is 10 years old)

Riad Sattouf

Racism

My dad says there's lots of violence in free schools. That's why he sends me to a private school. He's worried about me (I love him).

This is me

Thankfully he doesn't know that there are fights in my school too

NG!

I know exactly what racism is. It's fear of people with colours.

It's not just that. It's also thinking that there are different races of human beings...

And that some are superior to others...

Yeah, my race is superior to Esther's, yo

My dad who I love

Being racist is the worst thing in the world.

If you ever become racist, I'll disown you!

Hee hee

My brother who's such an idiot that nobody cares what he says

In my school, it's mostly white people. But there is an Asian boy, for example (I don't know where exactly he's from, though). He's in Year 3 and NOBODY ever talks to him.

Come on Esther, we're going to play tag

He stays near the pillar at break time and just waits for it to end

I think I heard the teacher calling him Jean-Luc once

And there are also two brothers, one of them in Year 4 and the other in Year 5. They're always together when they play football and I think they're Arabs.

They're typical boys — just as stupid as the others

Fuck!

Fucking pass it!

Nobody is racist to them at school. Or not that I've ever seen.

GOAAAAAAAAAAL

BENZEMA, WHAT A SHOT!

They're really good at football

And then there's my second-best friend, Cassandra — she's Black. It's weird though, it's like she's racist against herself. It makes me sad.

I'm soooo ugly...

Shh, you know that's not true...

Yes it is, I'm Blaaack, it suuucks

We have hugs at break time

She has family problems: she doesn't know her father and her mother is all alone. I don't even know what I'd do if I didn't have my dad. I think I'd die.

My mum said that after I was born, my dad went back to Martinique because it was too cold for him in Paris.

I've never seen him since then.

Sometimes I wonder if he thinks about me. When it's sunny in Paris, I think maybe he'd like it here...

Then she cries a bit, and afterwards we talk about something else

I don't see why anybody cares about the colour of someone's skin. What matters in life is being beautiful.

I'm okay — I'm quite pretty

And to be beautiful, you have to be blonde and bendy.

Me at dance class

Legs movin- side to side smack it in the air

When I'm 18, I'll dye my hair

It doesn't matter if you're Chinese, Arab, white, Black or even fat, if you're blonde and bendy, you'll succeed.

Wave your hands side to side put it in the air

Best example: Beyoncé.

Blonde + very built + super-rich

Black + super-bendy

= perfect

(Based on a true story told by Esther, who is 10 years old)

Riad Sattouf

25

Eugenie

I like our apartment, even if I'd prefer to have a room of my own.

This is me with my family watching "It's Only TV"

They're funny

HAHA

HAHA BRILLIANT!

Okay, now for the yoghurt challenge

On Saturday, I went to my friend Eugenie's apartment. It's the biggest apartment I've ever seen. I think her parents are billionaires.

I need the toilet

Fifth door on the right!

They have houses everywhere. But it's funny, their places are always a mess.

Even in the bathroom!

When I came out of the bathroom, this is what I said to Eugenie.

Every time I come to your place, I think "How can they live in such a pigsty?"

Oh yeah? Well, every time I go to your place, I think "How can they live in a place smaller than our toilet?"

THAT IS THE WORST AND MOST HORRIBLE THING ANYONE HAS EVER SAID TO ME.

(Based on a true story told by Esther, who is 10 years old)

Riad Sattouf

Zits

My dad is very protective of me (which is normal, because he's my dad).

This is us in the bathroom →

He's afraid that I'll be harassed by boys. He's always asking me if any of the boys at school are bothering me. It's sweet.

Hey, what's that? Whoa, I think you might have... ZITS!

GASP!

Zits! That means I'll be a teenager soon!

Me and my friends are always playing at being teenagers. Teenagers are older than us. They go to the big school.

OH YEAH, THEY'RE JUST LIKE THE ONES MY SISTERS HAVE!

Cool, huh?

Cassandra and Eugenie

When we play at being teenagers, we go out at night to a place without parents and we do whatever we want, like dancing (the waltz, etc.) and romancing.

You're so beautiful

Truly sublime

We only play with other girls. The boys in my school are total bastards (sorry about the swear word, but it's true). For example, at break time on the day I got my zits, we were playing and this is what happened.

Hey geeks! So do you touch each other's tits?

?

The boy who said that is called Abdou. He's in Year 6. He used to be nice but recently he's been horrible – and all because he wears a sleeveless leather jacket.

MIND YOUR OWN BUSINESS! GO AWAY!

You should tie your hair back, buy some clothes!

Make an effort! Wear leggings so we can see your arse! Ha ha!

All the boys dress like him

Abdou keeps bothering me. He's always saying stuff about love and dicks and I don't care about any of that.

Can I dance with you? It's better with a boy than with a girl...

Dancing real close...

Ha ha

MIIIISSSS THEY'RE HARASSING US! MIIISSS!

SHUT YOUR MOUTH, IDIOT! WITH YOUR TWO NIPS ON YOUR FOREHEAD!

I'M DOING YOU A FAVOUR!

How was school today?

Nips are what women have at the ends of their breasts, if you didn't know.

(Based on a true story told by Esther, who is 10 years old)

Riad Sattouf

The Hundred Years War

I don't like school. All the things we learn are boring.

This is me with my new hairstyle (it's better, right?)

We have the ugliest teacher in France

At the moment, for example, we're doing the Hundred Years' War. It was a war (this thing where everybody hates each other and they fight) between the English and the French that lasted a hundred years.

People back then were really ugly

It's really annoying. I don't see the point of learning about stuff that happened so long ago.

Joan of Arc was 17 when she heard the voices of saints telling her to liberate France...

Take Joan of Arc, for example. She was a woman with a terrible haircut and she heard voices telling her to kill the English, so she did.

JOAN! GO KILL THE ENGLISH PLEASE!

Um... okay.

Completely crazy

Then she commanded an army. They were all men and they all obeyed her! Boys obeying a girl? Yeah, like THAT's believable.

Go on!

ATTACK!

We must obey! Her hair's so cool...

And after that, I don't really understand all this, but Joan had to help the dolphin Charles to become king. But that can't be right, can it? Dolphins live in the sea! Anyway...

Come on, we're off to Reims!

EEK EEK EEK

Joan of Arc won all the fights and killed the English, just like the voices told her, and she became the most popular girl in France despite her haircut.

GASP it's Joan of Arc! I wish I was her friend...

But after that, things went wrong and she was burned alive while people laughed their heads off! I mean, I may not like her, but that's a bit harsh.

Apparently, the people who did that later apologized.

Sorry I laughed, I was just nervous

... and that's why Joan of Arc is known as "the mother of the French nation"

Then Kalila asked a really interesting question.

Yes, Kalila?

Miss, there's something weird about the Hundred Years' War in our history book, because it never talks about the Rebeus or the Renois... Did they do it on purpose not to mention them? Because there must have been some in the army and the cities and all that...

So maybe they did all the fighting really and Joan of Arc was a racist and she said "Yeah, we're not gonna mention them, let's just say it was us..."

Thank you, Kalila... I... Let's come back to that later...

And that's why I don't like school. We never talk about the really interesting stuff.

(Based on a true story told by Esther, who is 10 years old)

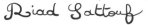

The Future

(Based on a true story told by Esther, who is 10 years old)

Riad Sattouf

Pretty Ill

We're a really happy family. We don't have any problems, to be honest.

I was pretty ill this week, and that made me happy.

I love it when I get ill because everybody looks after me. Well, my dad mostly.

The doctor came and he said what it was...

I also like being ill because I don't have to go to school. And this year, for the first time, I stayed at home alone. I could watch episodes of "Violetta" all day long.

It's an amazing show about the adventures of Violetta, this girl who becomes a singer like her dead mother.

"Violetta" is so exciting. It's about life and betrayal (and they all have iPhones too).

But the funniest thing about being ill is my brother.

It's always the same. He repeats the same stuff endlessly and thinks he's so clever...

Esther, can I ask you a favour? If you die, please come back and haunt our house! I really want to see something paranormal for once in my life.

I do it every time and I swear he doesn't even realize.

(Based on a true story told by Esther, who is 10 years old)

Riad Sattouf

The Killer Nutmeg Game

Panel 1: The person who makes me laugh most in the world is my dad.

He's brilliant at impressions →
HA HA HA!
Bonchour, I'm Nicolas Sarkauzi
NOTATALLFUNNY.COM
My idiot brother →

Panel 2: I like laughing. It helps me deal with life at my private school.

Footballer hair isn't allowed at my school.
I'm the poorest one there. Everybody else has a smartphone

Panel 3: When I finish Year 6, I'm supposed to go to the same free school as my brother. There aren't any private secondary schools around here.

My brother's practically the only boy in his school who doesn't have footballer hair
Because my dad won't let him

Panel 4: So yeah, I'm supposed to go to the same school as him when I'm older.

They'll rip you to pieces! That school is the worst place in the world!

Panel 5: My brother thinks he can scare me with his stories about the free school.

Ever heard of the killer nutmeg game? It's soooo cool!

Panel 6: "It's this game that everybody plays, even girls... First, people stare each other out in the playground..."

Panel 7: "They get together and wait till there are no monitors around. Then they go upstairs and stand in a circle. They put a tube of glue on the ground and open their legs."

Panel 8: "Then they take it in turns to try to kick the tube of glue between the legs of another player. You have to close your legs really quickly."

PUK

Panel 9: "Whoever gets the tube of glue between his legs... has to let the others beat him up until he passes out."

"Three kids have gone into a coma this year. Scary, eh?"

Panel 10: I wasn't scared by this at all. In fact, I challenged Antoine to play the killer nutmeg game with me.

He lost, of course. He's not quick or bendy at all!
PUK

Panel 11: ANTOINE! YOU LOST! NOW YOU HAVE TO LET ME BEAT YOU UP!
Yeah, right...
Go screw yourse...

Panel 12:

YAA!
ARGH!

Sorry, but life doesn't scare me one bit.

(Based on a true story told by Esther, who is 10 years old)
Riad Sattouf

Youpaurne

I'm a pretty under-standing person, but I'll never understand boys.

This is me thinking about my dad as I arrive at school

A Year 2 kid (who cares)

Today, for example, I was in the playground with Eugenie and Cassandra and we were talking about "Violetta" (only the best TV show in the world)...

He betrayed Violetta's trust

That's really bad, yo

... and then we saw the teacher running up to three boys: Louis (my ex-husband), Maxime (the best-looking boy in school) and Abdou (who's sometimes nice).

Hey! No mobile phones at school!

Haha fuck

WHASSUP WE'RE JUST TRYING TO GET ON YOUPORN!

PFHA HA HA HA

Hee hee

The teacher made this really weird face, like it was the most terrible thing ever.

Hngn I... you...

Then she took them to the headmaster and he called their parents to come and fetch them!

What's YOUPAURNE?

Dunno, it must be a game...

Miss, what's YOUPAURNE?

DON'T START, ESTHER!

YOUPAURNE – YOUPAURNE – YOUPAURNE... YOUPAURNE? YOUPAURNE... YOUPAURNE... YOUPAURNE – YOUPAURNE – YOUPAURNE!...

Oh, by the way, does anyone know what YOUPAURNE is?

(Based on a true story told by Esther, who is 10 years old)

Riad Sattouf

YouPorn

Yesterday, Abdou, Louis and Maxime were punished because they went on "Youpaurne" at school.

This is my dad taking me to school
Me

I asked my parents what it was but they said they didn't know.

I love him SO much

My dad knows what it is, but he doesn't want to tell me! He can't hide anything from me – I'm his daughter. I felt sure they were talking about that with the teacher and some other parents.

?

I saw Eugenie (FYI: she has an iPhone 6 and I don't have a phone at all)

Esther, I have to tell you a secret!

I went on YouPorn on my phone yesterday, yo

It's this site full of videos of people making babies!

Eugenie saw a video of a girl who was being hit by the boy while they were making the baby! Too weird!

It was the most horrible thing I've ever seen!

I know what making babies is. It's when a man and a girl rub their... well, you get the idea.

OHH OHH OHH
OHH OHH OHH
Our neighbours are always making babies, but they don't have any children

Abdou, Maxime and Louis were told off by the headmaster and their parents were summoned to the school. But they're all very rich, so they don't care.

Hi Esther... We're going on YouPorn... You know what that is?

Oh yeah, "Youpaurne", that's good... go ahead... if you want to...

"OH YEAH, YOUPORN, THAT'S GOOD"?!? YOU KNOW IT!!!
YOU GO ON IT!!!
HA!

MMMMM ♥ Estherrrr!
♥ MMMMM ♥ that's hot

Afterwards, everybody said "Apparently, Esther goes on 'Youpaurne' too."

(Based on a true story told by Esther, who is 10 years old)

Riad Sattouf

33

The Rabbit

I adore my family.

My mum — My dad (who I love) — My brother Antoine (an idiot, obviously) — Me

My favourite moment in life is when I go to bed. I close my eyes, think about nice food, and fall asleep in five seconds flat.

Me eating Oreos that fall from the sky

Almost every night, I have the same dream

I'm walking in the mountains with my parents.

Me in a princess dress

Just then, a rabbit arrives.

Your Highness! I'm being chased by a hunter! Help me hide, please!

?

I hide it under my dress and then the hunter arrives.

God be praised!

Hello, Your Highness... You didn't happen to see a rabbit come this way, did you?

He looks like my dad but it's not him

No, no!
Are you sure?
Yes, yes!
A very small rabbit...

I have a feeling you're hiding something from me...

Me? Absolutely not

In the end he goes away and the little rabbit is saved!

Thank you, Your Highness! I owe you my life!

You're welcome, little rabbit! Be happy!

I used to love this dream...

... but last week, the rabbit did something else.

And to thank you, here's an iPhone 6!

It was amazing! I could go on the internet and everything!

Violetta

Then I woke up and I remembered that my dad didn't want me to have a phone until I went to secondary school. Life is a nightmare.

(Based on a true story told by Esther, who is 10 years old)

Riad Sattouf

The Film

This is me in my dad's arms.

Sometimes he carries me when I'm feeling tired

I'm allowed to watch films, especially Disney films.

♪ "Let it go, let it goooo" ♪

I know them all so well that I watch them upside down

The other day my parents weren't home and my brother decided to watch a film called "Taken".

Can I watch it with you?

NAH it's not for children, it's too violent

I begged him and finally he let me.

I'll show it to you, but don't tell Dad! This is a real film, yo!

I PROMISE!

IT WAS THE BEST FILM I'D EVER SEEN.

You don't know it? It's the story of an American teenager who wants to go on holiday in Paris with a friend. But her dad's against it – he's afraid to let her leave (obviously, because he's her dad).

Call me as soon as you get there!

Of course! Bye!

Paris here we come!

They're about to get on the plane

No sooner do they get to Paris than they're kidnapped by boys! But the girl just has time to call her dad.

Don't move, bitch

DAAAAD HELP!

When he finds out, the dad goes straight to Paris.

He's really angry because he used to be a policeman or something

Everybody in this film has a phone

And then he kills EVERYBODY so he can find his daughter. It's really scary but really nice too.

WHERE'S MY DAUGHTER?

Pleeease don't tell my parents

It's a film about boys and how they're all idiots.

WHERE'S MY DAUGHTER?

Kzzz

KZZZZZ

Anyway, at the end, the dad saves his daughter and it's wonderful.

My love

My baby

DAAAAD I LOVE YOU!

Calm down, we just went shopping

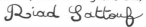

CASTORAM

We have to appreciate people while they're here because we never know what might happen to us in the future.

(Based on a true story told by Esther, who is 10 years old)

Riad Sattouf

Cassandra

This time, I have a very sad story to tell you. I've already told you about my lovely friend Cassandra. She lives with her mum in a high-rise outside town. Every day, Cassandra has to ride fifteen stations on the metro just to come to school. She's really really poor: she always wears the same clothes because her mum uses all her money to pay for school. And worst of all, Cassandra's dad abandoned her when she was one year old. He went back to live in Martinique because he couldn't stand the cold weather in Paris. Cassandra always talks about him when it's sunny here.

This is me and Eugenie

Cassandra

Her mum

The headmaster carrying Cassandra's schoolbag

She was all wet and she left a wet trail behind her

She walked through the playground like that, and apart from us, nobody looked at her. We didn't know that Cassandra's mum had come to fetch her from school because her dad... well, he died in Martinique. When she found out, Cassandra said "Can I go to the toilet?" So she went and, when she didn't come back out, her mum and the headmaster went to see what was happening. And, well, Cassandra... she'd tried to take her own life by putting her head in the toilet and flushing it. That was a week ago and she still hasn't come back to school.

(Based on a true story told by Esther, who is 10 years old)

Riad Sattouf

36

The Other Child

This is us having a family picnic.

We're in the Bois de Boulogne

So, there's something that... I didn't want to talk about it before but now I feel like I can, so I'm just going to say it.

Esther, would you like some grated carrots?

I told you a million times I hate them, don't you ever listen to me?

?

My mum is pregnant.

HEY, DON'T YOU DARE TALK TO ME LIKE THAT!

Be polite, sweetheart

Haha

Whoa, whassup!

Esther the OG

I didn't want to talk about it before because "she" didn't really exist, but now my mum's belly is starting to get big (bigger than normal, I mean).

I say "she" because I'm sure it will be a girl. Us girls have special powers for sensing that kind of thing.

Women are sensitive to the rhythms of the universe

We are receivers of information

I read that in a horoscope or something

In my imagination, my sister is nothing like me. She has curly red hair (not blonde – there are no blondes in our family).

She has thick hair

Small eyes

Round nose

Fat cheeks

Gap teeth

"Tomboy" type

Big feet

If it was a boy... well, that would be okay too...

Esther, can you tell me if my feet stink?

FLUB!

He'd be like my brother but smaller

HA HA HA HA!

HEE HEE HEE HEE HEE HEE

But a girl would be better.

This is my "flamenco" dress. It's my favourite.

WHOA!

IT'S BEAUTIFUL

I would be her role model. I'd teach her how to get popular at school...

You'll need a new hairstyle. But with hair like yours...

Never mind, my love, you'll just have to be "the funny one"

MWAH

And how is Daddy's sweet little baby?

Gni!

Actually I don't understand why my parents are having another child. But, I mean, it's okay. I'm fine with it.

(Based on a true story told by Esther, who is 10 years old)

Riad Sattouf

Kendji Girac

I'm a fan of Kendji Girac.

This is me with my new ponytail — it's better, right? →

♪ I caused her only sorrow when she wanted only love! I had her heart in my hands ♪

← Eugenie and me are singing "Elle m'a aimé" by Kendji

If you're old, you probably don't know Kendji Girac. He's THE favourite singer of all girls.

← Even more famous than Black M

He's so proud of his origins, you can see it in all his videos. I love his smile so much.

He shows us his life in the video of "Color Gitano" — it's very interesting →

You see him running along train tracks. It's really good.

He's with some friends, they're happy to be together

it's a way of life bigger than any country

Kendji Girac: 1 – he's a good singer. 2 – he's very good-looking. 3 – he's "sensual".

♪ I was just about to go home when I met you ♪

"Sensual" means he would rather move and dance than talk. This is an excerpt from his video "Conmigo" (I don't know what that means, I think it's Latin or something).

♪ I saw you coming to me, slow-motion beauty ♪

At the start, he's "chilling" with some friends

Then he sees some enemies.

♪ I couldn't move, I couldn't breathe ♪

And now he's feeling love for the girl who's with the enemies.

♪ Tell me what I have to do to make you mine ♪

She has the same hairstyle as me — funny, huh?

He looks at her, and what flows between them without talking... that's it, "sensual".

♪ Between us, the fire of desire ♪

She surrenders to him.

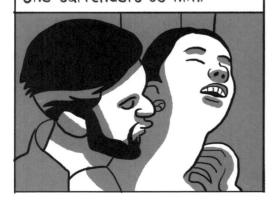

Anyway, if he doesn't know where to go next on his journey, he can always sleep here (just kidding).

♪ I don't want to bother you but you're under my skin ♪

♪ We could just chat Do you like to dance to romance Just stop thinking and let me entrance you ♪

(Based on a true story told by Esther, who is 10 years old)

Riad Sattouf

The Past

I can hardly remember anything from when I was very young. But I do remember a little bit. I remember being in my stroller with my dad. But in the memories of my mother, it's like she's all hair and no face.

Another time, I remember I was at the pool and my brother was annoying me, then Dad yelled at him and everybody was staring.

I remember a cartoon about Rapunzel called "Tangled Ever After". They were at the church and Rapunzel was about to marry Flynn. But Maximus (the horse) lost the wedding rings and didn't find them until the last second... That's my first film memory.

Oh, and I also remember one time we were on holiday in Bain-de-Bretagne and it was night-time. Me and my dad were in the garden and he'd just got the first iPhone. That was the first time I ever saw one.

(Based on a true story told by Esther, who is 10 years old)

Riad Sattouf

Gunfire

Last Sunday I heard gunfire on the street! So I looked out the window.

This is me, in "What's going on?" mode →

It was a boy throwing bangers

BANG! BANG!

His parents yelled at him in a foreign language. Everybody was watching from their windows. They were a really weird family.

The dad could hardly walk ↓

He'd been drinking, I think

BANG! BANG!

After a while, the dad sat down on the pavement and the mum shouted something and ran off.

BANG!

That was the only time the boy stopped throwing bangers. He went to see his dad and tried to help him up.

So the dad waved his hand like "get away from me" and the boy looked at me and I looked at him and I smiled and waved to be nice.

BANG!

THAT WAS A REALLY NASTY THING TO DO, DON'T YOU THINK?

(Based on a true story told by Esther, who is 10 years old)

Riad Sattouf

Sensitivity

Friday was the last day of school before the Easter holidays.

This is me sitting on my dad's back while he does push-ups

Yeah, my dad is super-strong

And on that Friday, Mitchell — one of the most horrible boys at my school — did another weird thing.

This is him with his shorts and socks (so ugly)

Nobody ever plays with him at break time, so he climbs onto a sort of bench near the wall and watches the street.

Waiting for break to end

So anyway on Friday he suddenly started screaming like a wild person.

AARRGH! AARRGH!

He sounded like a girl

Everybody went to see what his problem was.

HEEEELP! HEEEELP!

AARRGH!

He'd seen a pigeon get squished by a car just outside the school.

AAAARRRGH!

It was DIS-GUS-TING!

Mitchell started crying and calling for the teacher and stuff...

MISS! WE HAVE TO HELP HIM! HE'S HUUUURRRRT!

...and so everybody started laughing and making fun of him to make him cry even more...

YEAH HE'S SOOOO HURT, HE'S TORN TO FUCKING PIECES! QUEER!

HA HA HA HA HA   HA HA HA

VORTEX   ← Maxime's impersonation was so funny

...and we laughed and laughed.

HA HA MITCHELL HA HA

Sorry if you're shocked, but us kids... if a pigeon dies, we laugh. That's just how it is.

Come on, it's over now... He's gone to pigeon heaven...

HA HA

Our (super-ugly) teacher

Aheu! Aheu! Aheuuu!

And no, I'm not "heartless". For example, sometimes I imagine my dad dying...

Miss, something terrible has happened...

...your father is dead.

...and I immediately start crying. That's <u>sensitivity</u>.

He was sliced in half by a horse-drawn carriage.

Daddy...

(Based on a true story told by Esther, who is 10 years old)

Riad Sattouf

The Gym

This week, I went with my dad to the gym where he works.

This is me and him in the special changing room for employees

We're getting dressed in sports clothes

You need to wear sneakers that haven't been in the street

My dad is a really nice man. Honestly, even if he wasn't my dad, I'd still love him.

Hi Miguel, how are you? This is Esther, my princess

Hey Manu! How's it going?

He's a new teacher

Pleased to meet you, miss! What a beautiful girl — I bet she ends up a model.

Ha ha... she's got to finish school first

Everybody knows him. He's very popular. The customers all want him to themselves.

YO MANU!

All right, lads?

Could I have a word later?

But he treats everybody the same. He helps the super-sporty types...

Bend, Florence, down and then up again

UNGH

... and he helps people who go to the gym for the first time.

First, set a goal. What's your goal?

Um, to get muscly

But not too muscly

Okay, lads, the first thing you have to do is eat better to get rid of those bellies.

He makes them work their abs.

Aren't we hmmpf going to use the machines?

Until you get rid of that belly, the machines won't do you any good. Do another set of 15...

My dad is honest and sincere. There's a photo of him on a pillar in the gym.

He's just standing like that, between two walls in the corridor

He looks perfectly calm. Everybody can see that photo, and it shows them all that he's the strongest.

It brings tears to my eyes just looking at it

He's my dad and my role model. One day, I'll be like him.

For now, I can do this in my bathroom

(Based on a true story told by Esther, who is 10 years old)

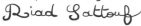

42

Little Bastard

I'm really sporty.

This is me doing the splits in our living room

I'm also very bendy

My dad loves sport (hardly surprising: he works in a gym), so we watch wrestling with him on TV.

My dad's really pleased when Antoine says that

Dad, I bet you could have been a professional wrestler

HA HA

Oh my God, he's challenging John Cena

Wrestling is men with big muscles fighting to see who's the strongest.

They always stare at each other angrily and say nasty things

They get into some really weird positions that hurt a lot. They're called "power moves".

YAHH!

COME ON SMASH HIM SMASH HIS FACE COME OOOOON! CRUSH HIM DAMN IT!

You dared to provoke me. You're going to regret it

My brother gets so excited when he watches wrestling and my dad thinks it's hilarious. He doesn't even tell Antoine off for swearing!

SMASH HIS STUPID BLOODY FACE THE BASTARD!

HAHA you know wrestling is all fake, right?

Afterwards, he usually wants to do the positions with me in our bedroom.

Little bastard loses!

Kh!

He calls me "little bastard" because one of the wrestlers on TV is a little person and that's his name.

Don't move, little bastard, or I'll do a "high-angle senton bomb"! You might die if you move!

He's getting ready, oh my God, he's climbed onto the top rope, he's going to destroy the little bastard, he's going to smash her!

WOAAAAAAAH

KRK

It really made this noise

He tried to avoid me at the last second, so he fell onto his knees and dislocated his menixus (that's what it's called).

But your knee braces make you look like a real wrestler!

He chose to hurt himself rather than me — that was nice of him!

And here's the Undertaker oh my God he's going to

(Based on a true story told by Esther, who is 10 years old)

Riad Sattouf

The Orphanage

The only times in life when I'm ever bored are in school. It's pretty sad.

This is me in class

This week, I got 5 out of 20 in math. Let's talk about something else...

My friend Cassandra came back to school. Her dad, who'd abandoned her when she was young, died in Martinique and she wanted to kill herself...

She was away a long time. We were happy to see her again. It's funny: the first game she wanted to play was the orphanage game!

C'mooon let's play it!

?

Seriously, yo?

The orphanage is a game we used to play in Year 4 (but we don't play it much any more). We're orphans and we go to an orphanage with a very strict headmistress.

You will obey because you have no family!

YES MIIIISSS!

Violet's good at being the headmistress

We have to follow all the rules and be very submissive.

Here you go, girls, you can eat the leftover dog food.

THANK YOU, MISS

You're too kind

Mmm!

But at night in the dormitory, one of us finds a hole in the wall.

Cassandra, where are you going?

I'm going to run away and hide in the forest!

Come back! That's not allowed! They'll whip you!

She goes to live "a natural life" in the forest.

Oh, the trees are full of fruit and if I get thirsty, I can drink river water...

Go back to sleep

This means a life of freedom, with no rules

I don't need anything. The forest will feed me!

She comes back at dawn and tries to convince the other orphans to go with her. So that's the game.

Run away with me! We can live freely, in nature!

No, we like the orphanage

It's too good for us!

When we played it before, none of the orphans wanted to leave. We all liked being good, obedient girls.

Go back to bed, the headmistress is coming!

What's going on?

Quick!

Come with me! I found a Samsung Galaxy Edge near the stream!

What?

Really cool phone

Her mum gave it to her to make her feel better after her dad died.

Everybody left the orphanage and we went to live "the natural life" in the bathroom with Cassandra.

Go ahead, I'll be the lookout...

GASP!

Whoa!

(Based on a true story told by Esther, who is 10 years old)

Riad Sattouf

Bad Girls

Abdou is a Year 6 boy who is sometimes nice and sometimes not (we don't know what's going on in his head). He's always talking about sex and stuff, he's obsessed, so anyway he was with his girlfriend and they were snogging in the toilets and then the other day they had a row and this is what he said.

GET AWAY FROM ME, YOU DIRTY HO!

Me   Eugenie   *We were really shocked* Cassandra   *Apparently Claire had cheated on Abdou with a boy from her after-school club*   *Abdou was really angry*

Aaaah, he called Claire a "DIR-TEE-HO"! That's bad, isn't it?   OMG   Did you see that?

Violet

I thought "dirty ho" was a bad way of saying "stupid idiot".

Nah, it's not that! My sister told me!

A "ho" is a girl who's so obsessed that she goes with lots of boys in exchange for presents or sometimes even money...

REALLY?

They're bad girls. Apparently only girls can be "hos". That's because we're not like boys.

Waaaaaah!

It'll be okay

See, girls are better than boys, because boys are obsessed. If a girl is obsessed, then she's just like a boy. There's nothing worse than that. So a ho is basically a boy.

I think that clears that up.

(Based on a true story told by Esther, who is 10 years old)

Riad Sattouf

45

Smells

I'm going to tell you about smells I like and smells I don't like.

This is me in "smelling my feet" mode

I don't like the smell of perfume. My mum wears it sometimes (Nina Richy is the brand).

It's like a billion crushed flowers in the air

Choking to death

I like the smell when I'm in my dad's arms. He smells of sweat, even when he wears Mennen (a brand of perfume for men).

It's like the smell of being perfectly safe or something

I don't like the smell of my brother in the bathroom.

Even with the door closed, it seeps through the cracks and it's like a solid poo smell attacking us

I like the smell of the metro just in front of the tunnel.

It smells of dry rubber and it's the smell of travel and adventure

I don't like the smell of alcohol.

Would you like to taste some good wine?

YUCKK

HA HA

It smells like dust but sour

I like the smell in the garage at my granny's house (we'll be going there soon).

It smells of smoke and cut grass and new trash bags

I don't like the smell of cheese (unless it's melted).

Sometimes I smell my dad's knife just after he's cut some goat's cheese and it smells of goat poo!

But I love the smell of four-cheese pizza from Pizza Pino.

It smells of oily warm food (yum)

I don't like the smell of steamed vegetables.

It's the smell of Sunday evening (I hate vegetables and school)

But the smell I love the best is the one that comes out of a brand-new iPhone box (I won't get one of my own until I go to secondary school).

My dad's iPhone box

sniff

It smells like nice, cool, welcoming plastic

The smell of happy days

(Based on a true story told by Esther, who is 10 years old)

Riad Sattouf

The Clown of Death

Just like every summer, we go to my granny's house in Bain-de-Bretagne at the start of the holidays.

There's not much to do there, but at least I get to see my friend Eugenie 2.

Her parents have separated since the last time I saw her and now she lives with just her mum in Nantes (I think that's in the south of France).

She told me that her mum works in a bar every night...

And I don't know if it's the neighbour or the Clown of Death...

Eugenie told me that when you brush your teeth in front of the mirror and look into your own eyes...

...but when you look at him, he vanishes

The Legless Lady is a dead woman (which is why she can't talk) who walks on two fleshy stumps and waits near your bed so she can stroke you with her long, soft, disgusting fingers.

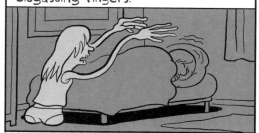

Now I'm in "scared to death" mode.

(Based on a true story told by Esther, who is 10 years old)

Riad Sattouf

The Police

One of the things I hate most in the world is dogs. I'm really scared of them.

This is me, being terrified

WOOF! WOOF!

I really really prefer cats.

Shifty eyes →

Drool →

Doesn't mind being on a leash (horrible)

Stink and shit (sorry for the swear word) →

← Impossible to know if they're nice or nasty

ROARR

Down boy

When we're in Brittany visiting Granny, we sometimes go to Saint-Malo. It's a town with a beach.

My dad

My pregnant mother
My brother

There are always dogs running around with no leashes.

Every time, they belong to old people with yellow hair and plastic jackets.

They hold the leash like this

And last time, this is what happened...

GRRRRR

Oww!

Then the old people told the police that my dad had beaten their dog. When really it was the dog that attacked me!

My dad explained that he'd been defending me, but the police didn't understand.

But he's on a leash, sir.

Yeah but he wasn't before...

At last they understood and went away. My dad told me that you always had to be polite to the police and explain things to them until they understood, even if they were a bit slow, because they could be dangerous.

I was so scared! All that because of a dog!

My dad quoted a line from a dead writer (called Jean Coco or something) about dogs.

"I prefer cats to dogs because there are no police cats."

↑ Really clever, right?

(Based on a true story told by Esther, who is 10 years old)

Riad Sattouf

The Taste of the Sea

I eat everything. Except anything that comes out of the sea.

This is me swimming in the sea (I like swimming, sometimes)

I hate fish, prawns, oysters, lobsters...

Grilled sea bream.

MMM!

YUCK!!!

My dad

I don't mind breaded fish, as long as it's really yellow...

...and nice and square.

What I really don't like is when you have to eat the whole animal.

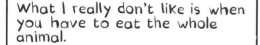

I see the poor thing suffering

I don't mind meat. You don't get this on your plate

But oysters are the worst.

You have to squeeze lemon juice on them to see if they're alive... They move, look!

My brother Antoine

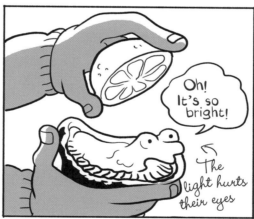

Oh! It's so bright!

The light hurts their eyes

ARGH IT BURNS

And the sea is really dirty. Yesterday, we were at the beach and my brother needed to go to the toilet.

Just go in the sea. It's not a big deal.

Ahhhhh!

HAHA! Feel better?

The fish will be pleased.

Yeah ha ha

How can anyone eat a creature that feeds on Antoine's poo?

(Based on a true story told by Esther, who is 10 years old)

Riad Sattouf

The Dead Singer

At my granny's house, I discovered an unknown French singer with the most beautiful voice. His name was Daniel Balavoine. My grandmother had all his albums. He was a sensitive, misunderstood artist who lived a long time ago.

Here he is on this poster that Granny gave me. Okay, he's not very good-looking (a little chubby) but that's why I get so emotional about him. He hated himself and he wanted to be loved

This song is called "Le Chanteur". It's about his dreams

Music was his world

And everywhere in the street
I want them to talk about me
I want naked girls
To throw themselves at me
To admire me and to kill me
To take my virginity
I want to be an idol
For the girls at my old school
Every night I want them
Breathless in their beds
To cheat on their husbands with me
Endlessly in their dreams

DANIEL BALAVOINE

I can't stop crying when I listen to these lyrics

I don't understand why he's not more famous

One day in Africa, he got in a helicopter because another passenger was late and the helicopter crashed. It's horrible but he DIED, just like that. Without ever achieving his dreams. It's so unfair! I really hope I don't die before I achieve my dreams (make at least one album and perform at least one stadium concert).

(Based on a true story told by Esther, who is 10 years old)

Riad Sattouf

Lucio

After Brittany, I went to a summer camp, like I do every year.

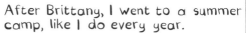

This is me telling my dad it's nice of him but he doesn't have to come with me all the way to the door of the train

TABAC

The camp is a place where there are just kids and no parents and we can do activities.

TAKE CARE, DAD!

Eugenie came with me. It was her first time!

And this year, at the station, something wonderful happened...

We were waiting on the platform with loads of other campers

... a boy came over to speak to me.

Yo, you're gonna find out what **LUCIO** thinks of you later.

HUH? Who?

He left, and another boy appeared...

Hey skirt! **LUCIO** wants to talk to you. He wants to tell you something 'bout you and him.

... and then a girl took me by the hand...

LUCIO told me to come and get you.

... and led me over to this mysterious boy... who was only the best-looking boy I've ever seen!

Excellent cap

"Diamond" earring

Expensive American-style jacket

Cool-dude hand movements

Yo, just wanted to tell you that you're the freshest girl in this train station

"Fresh" means really beautiful

← He was at least 12 years old!!!

Suddenly I felt overwhelmed...

You got a 6?

Um actually no but

He'd seen me from a distance

We didn't know each other! →

HE KISSED ME ON **THE MOUTH!**

...then he caught his train and I caught mine. I gave him my dad's number so he could send me the selfie we took before we said goodbye.

Our affair lasted less than 45 minutes.

Our goodbye selfie

(Based on a true story told by Esther, who is 10 years old)

Riad Sattouf

Enzo

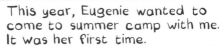

This year, Eugenie wanted to come to summer camp with me. It was her first time.

This is us trying to watch a Kendji video but the reception on the train was bad

I like going to summer camp because you meet new people. For example, this time I met Romane, a girl who loves to sing!

I smoke big joints and almost choke! Got two left I stuff 'em full and smoke!

HAHA THAT'S FUNNY!

She's singing a track by Jul (he's a rapper) in "crazy" mode.

The boys here are not like the ones at my school. They all have footballer hair for a start.

They keep walking up and down the corridor like they have somewhere to go

I'll smash him

GO 'HEAD YO!

They talk with an accent like rappers and they only ever talk about fighting.

FUCK DAT DUDE WHATCHA WAITING FOR?

AN' HE SAID TO ME "YO, YOU LOOKIN' FOR TROUBLE?" FUCK HIS HO MAMA!

He's wearing a hoodie even though it's hot

Oh, and they're also really trashy and obsessed (even more than the boys at my school, I mean).

Excuse me, I wanted to ask you...

Do you think you're a good kisser?

Lick my tongue and I'll give you my opinion

LET ME GO!

HEY MOFO WHATCHA DOIN'? DON'T TOUCH HER, YO!

CHIIILLL

Don't worry, Enzo's just being a dick cos everybody calls him Pogba cos he looks like Pogba and he thinks he's as popular as Pogba but he ain't no Pogba..

yo

"Pogba" is a very rich footballer

When we got to the camp, they told us that we'd be put in rooms for two.

When you've found your roomie, go over there.

Wanna be with me?

YEAAH!

Eugenie didn't understand. She thought we would be in the same room together.

Listen, we see each other all year. We can take a break for two weeks, don't you think?

You know girls like me make boys like you cry You think you can handle me at first, and that's fiiine...

Brilliant impersonation of Vitaa singing "Game Over"

Romane is just great.

(Based on a true story told by Esther, who is 10 years old)

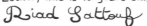

52

Ormythology

The summer camp is in Arcachon (which is near Brittany, I think).

This is me and Romane, my cool new friend

Heyyy

The monitors

What's great about camp is that they have tons of different activities every day.

Who you thinking 'bout when I come in on the beeeeat?

She sings "Game Over" all day long, it's so cool

For example, we go out to look at birds. It's called ormythology.

Now tell me who puts the pressure on the beeeeat!

KWAK! KWAK!

Birds are creatures with wings and they fly (I think everybody knows that).

By the way, the monitor has a tattoo on her back and I keep wondering how far down it goes

We saw a sort of big white bird with a long straight neck that used to be a dinosaur (the guide told us that) but I can't remember its name.

Yeah, that's what I saw

Yes, it really did have a tail

And I swear you could see its teeth

Anybody know what it's called?

Birds have eyes on either side. They don't see ahead like we do. That means they look sideways as they go forwards.

Poor things

It's really difficult — I tried

We were interested but we didn't see much. It was mostly just seagulls.

Here's one

At one point, a small blue bird flew past really fast. But the guide was chatting with the monitor and he didn't see it.

HEY, IT'S A KINGFISHER! A FREAKING KINGFISHER, YO!

This is Enzo but everybody calls him Pogba

Whassup, man? Whaddja see?

A KINGFISHER! THERE WAS A KINGFISHER!

It's true, sir. We saw it too!

Finally the guide saw it too and everybody was happy because it's a really beautiful bird.

It looked at us

Super-cute

I really wish I could have one in my bedroom in Paris

It's weird that Enzo knows the names of birds and all that, don't you think? What a geek

Yeah, totally

(Based on a true story told by Esther, who is 10 years old)

Riad Sattouf

Rachida

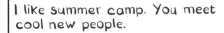

(Based on a true story told by Esther, who is 10 years old)

Riad Sattouf

Dance Night

You have to pay for summer camp, even if most of the kids there are from free schools. This year, I met some really great people, for example my new best friend Romane (her real name's Rachida, but she wants everybody to call her Romane). On the last night, the monitors organised a dance and we were allowed to choose the music ourselves.

(Based on a true story told by Esther, who is 10 years old)

Very Sad Days

Here's something I've noticed: sometimes in life you have happy days and sometimes you have very sad days.

This is me leaving summer camp with my new friend Romane

I got so upset when we said goodbye (even if we agreed that we'd see each other again)...

My dad

Well, it's nice to see that you're happy to be home!

Nobody came to fetch her. She went on the metro all alone →

To make me feel better, my dad (who I love so much, and yes, I do tell him) bought me the three things I most love to eat (apart from four-cheese pizza from Pizza Pino)!

Food is very important to me

You're the best, Dad!

First I had Zapetti ravioli. Heaven in a tin.

A whole can just for me!

Yum yum

I like it when my dad opens the tin. This delicious smell comes out — the smell of Italy.

SNFF

Pizza, ravioli... yeah, I love Italian food!

I like to eat three or four cold ravioli straight from the tin, before warming up the rest.

You can really smell the tomato when it's cold

And the sauce is thicker

You're looking happier already

For dessert, my dad bought me my favourite fruit: a giant yellow mango.

It weighed at least two pounds (all for me!)

What I like best is when I scrape the inside of the skin with my teeth. You get all these juicy yellow threads.

I save the stone for last

But best of all was the big bag of sour lime-flavoured Head Bangers (my favourite sweets in the world).

They're so sour that I wonder if they might be dangerous

They give me a shock every time.

KRAK

I wonder if anybody has thought of making super-sour mango ravioli (I don't know why I said that, I must be going crazy).

XZSCHK

My mum is at my grandmother's house and my brother's at camp, but I miss Romane more than either of them.

Is it life or the sweets that are making me cry? I don't know

(I finished the whole bag of Head Bangers in one night.)

(Based on a true story told by Esther, who is 10 years old)

Fly Minerate

I'm in "holiday" mode at the moment, but the holidays are ending.

This is me staring sadly through my window at the rain falling on Paris

There was a big problem this week, when my dad went to the train station to pick up Antoine (he'd been at summer camp).

YOU'RE A PAIN IN THE ARSE! YOU HEAR ME? I'M SICK OF YOU!

Hey, it's my body I can do what I want I don't give a crap what you...

I'd never seen my dad this annoyed before!

IN MY HOUSE YOU'D BETTER GIVE A CRAP, BOY!

He was in "fight" mode

My brother had got a footballer haircut during summer camp!

My dad had always told him not to get his hair cut like that. He said it was the devil's haircut

All boys love football and they've got "Fly Minerate" or something written on the shirt. I don't even know what that means

He had the same hairstyle and shirt as his hero Jérémy Ménez (he's a footballer)

Before summer camp, he looked like this

He doesn't just look stupid, he really is

My dad called the summer camp and yelled at them that he wanted his money back.

I won't tell you everything that happened, but my dad smashed my brother's headphones against the wall to punish him.

He cried so much, I felt sorry for him

There was a mark on the wall

After that, he wore sunglasses and stayed up all night on his phone. Weird

I think I might wait till next week before I tell my dad that I want a new look too...

(Based on a true story told by Esther, who is 10 years old)

Riad Sattouf

57

Breasts

And now the holidays are over. Actually, I always enjoy going back to school. It's like a new start.

Cool, yo!

This is me with my new look

Think: hip, sporty, bendy

I changed a lot this summer (I've been through some stuff). I like the "dynamism" of my new outfit.

Cap on backwards because it's fun to bend the rules a bit

I'm in Year 6 now. I'm one of the big kids.

Here, Dad, I don't think I'll wear it after all

At the last minute, I just decided the cap was a bit too much

Everybody had a new look — it was funny!

HEY BABE!

Hee Hee

Cassandra had a new hairstyle!

I was so happy to see her again

So, anyway, I saw all my friends again, but I think it's over with Eugenie.

HI THERE!

!

She has a new look too

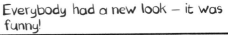

She said hello to Cassandra and totally blanked me

We didn't really hang out at the summer camp in July and we haven't been in touch since.

She's acting like she thinks she's a teenager already

Then we met our new teacher, who is just really weird.

I'm Mishuzh Rodriguezhhh mmm. Everybody in line pleazhe mmm

She's not actually a little person, she's just really short.

Ready, girlzh and boyzh mmm? Then letsh go mmm

Yep, she's the same height as me

Honestly, where does this school find its teachers? After ten minutes, I'd had it with her "mmms" at the end of every sentence.

Mrs Rodriguez

You can jusht call me mish mmm

They've mixed us all up, so I don't know many people in my class. Only Cassandra, Eugenie, Mitchell and two others.

Mitchell, the worst boy in the class, hasn't changed at all unfortunately

Eugenie sat at the front. She took off her jacket and turned to me. I saw pure hate in her eyes. I was really shocked.

She was in "enemy" mode

Oh, and another shock: SHE HAS BREASTS NOW

(Based on a true story told by Esther, who is 10 years old)

Riad Sattouf

58

Part 2
Tales from My 11-Year-Old Life

Back to School

My name is Esther and I'm 10 years old. I'm in Year 6 at a private school in Paris.

This is me and my best friend Cassandra at break time

Life at school is very different this year.

Most of the students are new

There are three groups in my class now. The "runts", the "normals" and the "bad boys".

Me and Cassandra are "normals": we play games and we use swear words, but not all the time.

SHIIIIT! I messed up!

Yup

The "runts" of the class are the ones who are, you know, a bit strange. Like Mitchell, for example.

He still stares out at the street and now he wears his hair in a ponytail sometimes, even though he's a boy

His trousers are still too short

There's also Marina, who spends all her time playing with an imaginary friend.

We'll be playing and she'll wander off, talking to herself

Yes Hector, let's go see Dad ...

Us in "What the...?" mode

And then there's Arthur who does weird things with his mouth.

This is the movement his mouth makes over and over again all day long

PWUH

① ② ③

The "bad boys" are a group of kids who have loads of lovers and use loads of swear words. Everybody else wants to be like them (except me).

Lucas, their leader

Cool-dude hand movements

Louis, my ex-husband

Yep, girls can be bad boys too

This is Lina

And guess what! Eugenie, my ex-best friend, is now one of the bad kids. She's Lucas's girlfriend!

An' then, right, he sez, "Yo, your mother's a ho," and I'm like "You fucking what, dickhead? What didja say?"

They talk in show-off voices

Go on, say it again, prick!

It's weird, Eugenie didn't used to care about love at all but now she's obsessed (it's because she's got breasts, I think).

But we're not allowed to use phones – the teacher will tell you off, yo

HAHA who gives a fuck? Screw that, ho

I could never swear like that

I don't know if you remember Maxime, the rich kid who was the most popular boy in school last year? He fell off a rock in Corsica this summer and spent two months in hospital.

He was like this in Year 5

Now he's like this

He used to be the coolest dude and now he's one of the runts. Crazy, huh?

Nobody talks to him any more

He just sits there hugging himself, staring at the others and smiling

(Based on a true story told by Esther A, who is 10 years old)

Chouchous

This week, we chose our chouchous for the year.

This is me getting my hair braided by Cassandra

A chouchou is a scrunchy

But that's not the kind of chouchou I mean

Every year, new Year 2 kids join the school.

Ha ha, look at them!

They're all really tiny, so they're scared of everything.

They cry because they miss their parents or something

And the boys like to beat them up for no reason.

OWW!

WHAT THE HELL! WHY DID YOU DO THAT?

DO WHAT? I DIDN'T TOUCH HIM!

UGH

So the school encourages the bigger kids (Year 5 and Year 6) to choose a chouchou – a favourite – that they can protect and teach about life and stuff.

This is us deciding which ones to choose

So I chose this really cute little girl, and you know what she said to me when I told her she was going to be my chouchou?

Like a little doll

I DON'T WANT TO BE YOURRR CHOUCHOU, I WANT TO BE HERRR CHOUCHOU BECAUSE HER HAIRRR IS SO BEAUTIFUL!

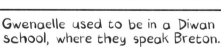

It was the best day of Cassandra's life.

LA LA LA

They're inseparable now

So in the end I didn't choose a chouchou, the teacher gave one to me. Her name is Gwenaëlle.

Esther's granny is from Brittany, just like you!

Gwenaëlle used to be in a Diwan school, where they speak Breton.

Hi there! Welcome to Paris!

Look at her hoodie!

Esther! Te zo ken koantig hag ur galon!

SOMEBODY SAVE ME PLEASE

(Based on a true story told by Esther A, who is 10 years old)

Riad Sattouf

62

Joy

I'm a pretty good student (not the best, not the worst, but better than average).

It's the weekend!

YAY!

Me and my dad on the street in "Friday" mode

You know what I don't think people talk about enough? Joy.

When I listen to "J'écoute du Miles Davis" by Navii (this singer who's kind of girly but cute and looks a bit like Kendji), I feel filled with joy

My pain at the bottom of a bottle because we won't be together any more

Joy is simple: it's when life gives us pleasure and we feel good. It's the best thing ever.

It's like how your heart leaps and slowly falls again when Navii is followed by Daniel Balavoine's "Sauver l'amour" on your playlist

Going to the Ganges to erase my pain

My dad makes me joyful. When he looks at me, I know everything is going to be okay.

Nope, I still don't have a phone

For example, here, he's letting me use his iPhone and I go on Wikipedia (a site that knows everything there is to know) to find out if Jupiter (the planet) is made of rocks or gas.

I can tell he's proud of me for being a good student and that gives me joy

Gas! Now can I look at Venus?

Sure

Last time at my dance class we did a routine to "Avenir" by Louane (a singer I like, except for her nose).

WAH OH ♪ WAH OH WAH OH OH ♪ WAH OH WAH WAH OH OH ♪ WAH ♪ OH WAH

I was singing and dancing and doing my moves...

I hope that you suffer

And that you can't sleep

...and I was so good, I was like a professional or something...

In the meantime, I'm going to write For tomorrow, for the future! For tomorrow, for the future!

Filled with joy

The other day, there was some apple juice in the fridge. My mum told me to finish it because she'd opened it two weeks ago and she was worried it would go bad.

But the carton was almost full. I don't think she realized!

Apple juice is dee-lish-uss

I drank the whole thing! My mum thought it was just a mouthful, but it was nearly a litre.

My head was spinning with joy and a sugar rush

Joy isn't always just a good feeling. For example, when my brother starts insulting me and my dad shuts him up with a look and a single word.

Come on, pass the mayo, you h...

HEY...

He stops straight away because he doesn't want to die

Krch Krch

AND I FEEL A SORT OF EVIL JOY

(Based on a true story told by Esther A, who is 10 years old)

Riad Sattouf

63

Teeth

I'm 10 years old and I've already lost 21 teeth!

This is me with my teeth on my chest (my dad keeps some of them in a box at my granny's house)

Teeth are hard white things that grow in your mouth. You use them to eat (and smile).

Yep, this little thing was in my mouth and now it isn't (and yep, nobody cares except my dad)

When you're a child, you have milk teeth and they fall out one by one and other teeth replace them.

This horrible photo of me is from a long time ago. Please don't show it to anybody

I'm always losing my teeth in weird ways (typical me).

One day I was drinking through a straw and watching a film and I accidentally got my tooth caught in the straw

You think that Shrek is your true love?

It was stuck in there so hard, I couldn't get it out again after!

Well... yes! Ha ha ha ha ha ha!

Another time, I was reading a book at my granny's house and my mum gave me a surprise kiss (we do that in our family — my mum's idea)...

Another time, I gave my dad a kiss that made a PFRTTT noise on his belly...

And another time, my brother knocked me out of the hammock in my grandmother's garden...

WHAAT? I'M ALLOWED IN THE HAMMOCK TOO!

I really like my new teeth. They have these little waves on them.

I'm a bit tense here because I'm at the dentist. I'm not scared of her though — she never hurts me and she's really pretty too. Anyway, this is what she said:

Your canines are a little too friendly with your lateral incisors! We're going to have to separate them a bit

So I'm going to have a thing on my teeth like my ugly brother.

Heyy, Esther's got braces! Ha ha you're going to SUFFER now bee-yitch!

The dentist told me "Come back in June so I can fit it." Since then, I pray (yes, pray!) to God every night, asking him to take pity on me.

Dear Lord, it's fine to make me suffer because I'm not afraid of suffering. But please please don't let the braces make me uglier than I am. Also, next year I go to secondary school, and if I could stay just a teeeensy bit popular, that would be really great...

(Based on a true story told by Esther A, who is 10 years old)

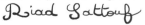
Riad Sattouf

Les Marseillais

I love the weekend. You can relax, have some time to yourself, and hang out with friends away from school in "no stress" mode.

This is my mum

And me

Cassandra's mum

See you tonight!

My best friend Cassandra

I love Cassandra and I feel so bad for her. Her dad died last year and her mum is poor.

But despite all that, she laughs and sings and enjoys life

YAYY

Oreos, yum!

I would just cry all day if my dad died.

It makes me want to be super-loving with her

Your bedroom is great

Cassandra's mum asked my mum if Cassandra could stay with us on Saturday afternoons while she was working in a shop.

Cassandra is a pretty good student but she doesn't like to read. I'm the opposite – reading is my passion

I should pass it on to her

When she's at home, she watches television all day (she loves reality TV shows).

How about we read "The Baby-Sitters Club"? It's really good

Ugh, no, let's just watch "Les Marseillais"

I'm not allowed to watch TV...

Who cares? We can watch it on my phone ha ha ha

"Les Marseillais" is a programme about real people who want to work in nightclubs and stuff, and they're all from a city called Marseille.

The people in that city have a weird way of talking

C'MON EH!

NAH

For example, they say "Watchatelliimeh" instead of "What did you tell him?" It's hard to understand, but it's still very interesting because it's about "youth" issues.

I'd like him to esplain why he kissed Rawell

Watwazatabouteh?

But he won't tell me

The boys are really sporty and they're always in "chill" mode.

And they're always in their underwear – mmm (just kidding)

C'MON EH

Nah I toldja

Cassandra's favourite is a beautiful girl who's Renoi (that means "Black") like her. She's a booking agent or something. She's in charge of the show – she gives the candidates jobs, and sometimes she fires them.

OMG she's so beautiful

You're fired – leave now

So anyway we were watching it and then my mum came in and she talked to Cassandra.

You know, reading is really great! The words conjure images and sounds in your head... Don't you want to put your phone down and use your imagination?

Not really, thanks

On TV there are images and words... In books, there are just words, so many words. That's why I prefer TV. Sorry. I'm just really not interested in imagining stuff. I'd rather SEE it.

I'll be honest: Cassandra is right about the images and the sound and all that. TV is better than books. But when you're not allowed to watch it, like me, then you're really thankful that books exist...

(Based on a true story told by Esther A, who is 10 years old)

The Election

I'm going to tell you about the election of our class delegates.

This is me when I found out that there was going to be an election that afternoon (I was happy because it meant no work)

YAYY!

Elections are democracy. That means that each of us has to write the name of the candidate they like best on a bit of paper and the one with the most votes is "elected" (that means chosen).

In order to ensure the neutrality of the election, the candidates will be anonymous. Everybody will have a chance

Delegates are students who represent the other students and help them talk to the teacher and the headmaster or something.

So each candidate will write a manifesto and I'll read them out

You'll vote for the speech you like best. The words are more important than the people

So everybody who wanted to wrote a little speech and put it in a box with a hole at the top.

I didn't bother — I'd rather be free

Plus I'm a bit of a loner and a dreamer

The teacher read out the speeches. There was a bit of everything...

"If you vote for me, I promise to do all I can to get us some football goals with real nets, and for people who prefer basketball, a new net for the hoop..."

Definitely a boy

It's funny — some of them really want to get elected but they don't actually promise anything.

"Please vote for me! If you vote for me, I'll be so happy, so please will you please vote for me? Please. Thank you."

One of the speeches said: "A vote for me is a vote for pizza" because he was going to ask for pizza four times a week at the cafeteria. Everybody wanted to vote for that one!

The teacher said "That's not going to happen"

HEY what about democracy, miss?

It was his speech

What a joke! Seriously, what's the point?

Lucas said in his speech, "If I'm the delegate, I'll share my cards with all of you..."

He made a little sign so that everybody would know it was his speech. The cheat!

He means his Yu-Gi-Oh! cards

Everybody saw him, and since he's very rich, everybody voted for him to get some cards. But when he realized he was going to get elected, he said this:

Well actually I don't have enough cards for everybody, so I'm not going to give them out. But thanks for voting for me!

What a scam!

The teacher let him get away with it. She said: "It was an electoral promise, you believed it, you voted, end of story."

HE CHEATED MISS! HE SAID WHO HE WAS!

I didn't see anything!

I'M GOING TO TELL MY MUM!

The other speech that was elected was a speech that said, "Vote for me and I'll use your ideas, I'll listen to you, and I'll fight for us to be allowed to wear uniforms and stuff..." I voted for that one (uniforms are cool).

And in fact it was a girl called Athena who everybody hates!!!

She's really the worst: she looks like a boy, and when people ask her if she's an intellectual or something, she says "Yes"! Honestly, it was horrible when we realized that she was the delegate.

Everybody started booing but it was too late

She smiled like this

(Based on a true story told by Esther A, who is 10 years old)

Riad Sattouf

Electoral Fraud

There are problems with the class delegates at the moment.

This is me listening to Lucas, one of the delegates, telling people his ideas

I'm going to ask for the playground to be named after Aimé Jacquet because he coached the French team that won the World Cup in '98, yo

Yeah man GREAT idea

Lucas lied and cheated to become a delegate, so Mathis (the candidate who wanted pizza four times a week) told his mum.

She asked to see the headmaster right away

Madame

She made an official complaint about electoral fraud and demanded new elections.

The headmaster refused because there was no proof of cheating (even though it's true – I saw him cheating!)

Hee hee

Mathis cried

The other delegate is this HORRIBLE girl. She won because the candidates were all anonymous. She's a very ugly person, on the outside AND the inside.

She promised to use our ideas, to look after us, and to ask for school uniforms "like in Japan"

When we found out it was her, we were all really upset

Of course, she didn't do any of the stuff she said she would. All she did was talk to the teacher and the headmaster and she never told us what they talked about! And we elected her!

And not only that, but look at her feet!

I saw them in PE

The feet of the female chimpanzee at the zoo are better than these, because, you know, at least they're <u>supposed</u> to be hands

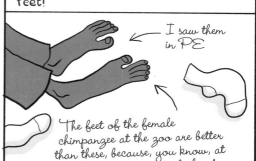

At our school there are loads of love affairs. That's just how it is. We get married, we get divorced, we laugh and we cry – that's life, right? The teachers don't like it, but they don't do anything about it. So Athena, instead of asking us for our ideas or campaigning for uniforms like she said she would, told the headmaster that the students had complained to her about the weddings, and that's NOT TRUE – she doesn't talk to any of us and we don't talk to her! So after that meeting with the "educationary staff" or whatever (the teachers, basically), she came out and said THIS:

Okay, so I've arranged it with the headmaster: no more weddings or love affairs. It's age-inappropriate and it's a disruptive influence.

From now on, love is forbidden.

Honestly, if she died right now and somebody told me, "Hey did you hear, Athena is dead?", I reckon I'd say, "Oh yeah?" and I'd go off to play Kemps (it's a card game).

(Based on a true story told by Esther A, who is 10 years old)

Paul and Arthur

(Based on a true story told by Esther A, who is 10 years old)

The Baby

Do you remember how I told you my mum was pregnant?

This is me putting my glass on her belly because it's funny

Take that off me

LOL

We walked over and I saw him!

Well, this week, she gave birth! It's weird though: I felt sure I was going to have a sister, but in fact the opposite happened.

We went to see them in the maternity ward (that's the part of the hospital where babies come out of bellies).

← *My dad brought some chocolate-covered pistachios*

My mum said the birth went well (it's because this is her third time and she's used to it) but she looked pretty tired.

The baby wasn't with my mum, he was in a little box at the end of the room →

Gaëtan, my little brother

His hair is so blond it looks like it's made of gold and there's loads of it (rare for a baby, apparently)

He's tiiiiny!

His hands are really perfect and his fingernails are almost microscopic

Pretty chubby

His feet look like they're made out of plastic

His mouth is unbelievable

We were all like this once

This is him awake (his eyes are small and they're super-blue)!

He's sleeping here. He doesn't move, which is scary, but Mum says it's normal

When he cries he's really ugly and he sounds like a puppy!

Prrrpffprrr

He purrs like a cat!

This is his normal expression, with his tongue hanging out like it's too big to fit in his mouth! Will he always look like that?

(Based on a true story told by Esther A, who is 10 years old)

Riad Sattouf

A Choice of Fathers

Panel 1: So now I have two brothers! There are five of us in the house.

This is me
It feels weird saying "I have two brothers" because the second one's only just been born
His name is Gaëtan

Panel 2: I'd love to have a child of my own.

My dad could crush his skull just by closing his hand

Panel 3: I can tell I'd be really good at looking after a baby.

Can I wear these gloves to change him so I don't get dirty?
NO!

Panel 4: I really adore my mum, but it's weird, I feel like she has nothing in common with my dad.

Hey calm down I was KIDDING!
She never gets my jokes

Panel 5: It's encouraging that somebody like her managed to find a man to have children with.

My feet were never on the grooouuund! If only I were a bird instead ohoooooohhh I don't belong in this body no
A song by Balavoine (an unknown singer) that I love to hum

Panel 6: I don't like Year 6 because nobody plays games any more.

At break time, the girls just wander around the playground and talk
Yeah, right?
Yeah
My ex-friend Eugenie

Panel 7: All they ever talk about is "who loves who" and "who's going out with who"...

And then he said "Yo, I love you"
What? Seriously?!
It gets boring after a while
And, you know, she didn't say anything because she doesn't want to be like "Yeah I'm sooo in love"

Panel 8: So I prefer to just sit in a corner on my own, with my three lovers (yep, three).

This is the SOS of an earthling in distress

Panel 9: They don't know there are three of them. They're all in different classes. One of them plays basketball.

That's him

Panel 10: The second one plays football with the third one.

They don't know they're right next to each other!

Panel 11: We never talk but we smile at each other and we know we're united by love.

Panel 12: I find it reassuring to know I have a choice of fathers. You know, for when I decide I want children.

(Based on a true story told by Esther A, who is 10 years old)

Riad Sattouf

Friday 13th November, 2015

Yesterday was Friday 13th. Apparently that's an unlucky day. My brother told me that there's even a horror film called that (a horror film is a film where loads of people are killed — I've never seen one). But I'm the opposite. I have the feeling that Friday 13th brings me good luck. Last night, my parents were watching a football match on TV (I hate football) and I was in my bedroom. I went to the kitchen to get a drink and when I arrived in the living room my dad turned off the TV and said, "Hey, why don't we watch 'Tangled'" (which used to be my favourite ever Disney film!). So we put it on.

(Based on a true story told by Esther A, who is 10 years old)

Riad Sattouf

71

Fear

When I got to school on Tuesday, everybody was really frightened.

This is me finding out that there'd been a terrorist attack in Paris

This is my friend Cassandra telling me about it

It happened the night we watched "Tangled".

Now I understand that my dad was hiding it from me so I wouldn't be upset

Cassandra spent the whole weekend watching TV

Terrorists are stupid idiots (sorry to be rude) who kill people that haven't done anything wrong.

The terrorists BLEW THEMSELVES UP to kill all those innocent people!

I don't understand why they do that. I heard that terrorists are happy to die because they believe that there are women waiting in heaven to make food for them or something.

So sad

It's hard to believe anybody could do such a terrible thing.

Cassandra being consoled by her Year 2 chouchou

I fired mine, so...

... I had nobody to console me

If they want to commit suicide so they can go to heaven, why don't they just do it in their bedroom? I don't understand why they kill other people too.

They must be scared to go there alone.

And the innocent people they killed hadn't even made fun of the terrorists' god like they did last time with the Charlie.

*This time, I didn't laugh once during the minute's silence**

Afterwards, everybody told stories about people they knew whose lives had been saved by their smartphones.

On my mother's life, I swear my grandfather was making a call in the street and a bullet exploded his phone! If he hadn't been holding it, he'd be dead, yo

Lucas, a cool dude

And then something totally freaky happened to me and Cassandra.

We left the school and there was a guy on a motorbike staring at us...

VRRRRR

... and he did this!

VROAR

Scared now, aren't you? CHABICHARIBARICHACHICHARI!

And he said something in a foreign language!

Waaaaah!

HA HA HA HA HA!

VROA

After he left, we just cried and cried.

(Based on a true story told by Esther A, who is 10 years old)

Riad Sattouf

*See Esther's Notebooks: Tales from my 10-year-old life

Secours Populaire

On the last day before the Christmas holidays, the teacher took us to a charity shop called Secours Populaire...

This is me laughing at how small Madame Rodriguez is

This is her — she really is tiny

We were on an outing

We each had to take one of our old toys so they could be given to a poor child.

I brought my Cicciobello...

Really? You didn't want to keep it?

It's a doll that talks if you put batteries in it

Pfft, it's a baby toy!

Secours Populaire is a charity where "volunteers" (people who aren't paid) work to help the needy.

I've got a little brother now so I don't need a doll

Anyway it's broken

The teacher is always talking to us about "all-true-ism", which means being nice and thinking about other people and helping those who aren't as lucky as us or something.

So the teacher gave a speech and so did the people from Secours Populaire, who were all wearing Father Christmas hats, but I didn't actually listen to it

I noticed that the teacher has a stud on her tongue!

Take out your toys now and put them on the table

Doesn't seem very "all-true" to pierce your tongue, but whatever

So anyway, when I put my Cicciobello on the table, she talked (the batteries still worked)!

SCHKRRR YUM YUM MAMA HUUUG

K RR

And then, well, I just burst into tears.

I felt like I was abandoning her or something

Works great — thanks!

KRR MAMA KRR

They gave us each a lollipop then, but since I was crying so hard I couldn't manage to open mine.

I didn't want to admit that I was crying about my doll (what a baby)

I see

pop

When the grown-ups saw me, I became the chouchou of Secours Populaire.

It's okay, love, we'll help you!

What's up?

It's not worth crying over!

When the grown-ups saw me, I became the chouchou of Secours Populaire.

Waaaaaah

MPF MPF MPF

And in fact it took all four of them to open it because the plastic was stuck.

They shouldn't make 'em so hard to open

Sniff

There!

How are kids supposed to manage that?

They managed in the end. It made me feel so much better that they all helped me. They're really nice people.

Thank you, Secours Populaire sniff

(Based on a true story told by Esther A, who is 10 years old)

Riad Sattouf

Binmen

I'm a "family" kind of girl. That means I like relaxing and doing nothing in our little cocoon.

This is me and my family in "happy" mode

Just being

Yep, my mum and dad read books. They have a bookshelf in the corridor, but they're all adult books (horror and politics, stuff like that).

My brother Antoine doesn't read, he just looks at his phone.

HEY, I do read! I read loads of websites, yo

Don't say I don't read

My brother is such a punk

I read!

I'm really into reading this year. It all began with "Little Women", which my granny bought for me.

It's the story of four sisters, their mother and their faithful servant who try to manage while the father is out at the war being a doctor

Farewell my daughters, duty calls...

My favourite character is Jo March because she's fearless and she has long black hair like me.

I WANT TO GO TO WAR TOO! BUT I CAN'T BECAUSE I'M A WOMAN! IT'S NOT FAIR!

Come on Jo, why don't you help me make dinner instead?

I also really like "The Baby-Sitters Club". It's a series about some girls who form a club for babysitters and it works well and then they have adventures and help each other when they have problems looking after the kids.

I have a little brother, so I can relate to that

Hold him — he might fall off!

The character I like best is Kristy Thomas. She's great.

I like her name, it just sounds really cool

A rebel

Sporty, casual clothes like jeans and T-shirt, so she's ready for action

Bendy

She's just like me

At school they asked us what we wanted to do when we were older and I said "read books" because I love it so much.

Do you want to write them too?

Nah, not really, just read them...

You're right — writers don't get paid much. You could be an "editor"

REALLY?

Apparently, an editor is somebody who chooses what books to publish and sometimes you even give orders to writers so they write what you want, and then you sell them and you can get very rich! Sounds AMAZING, right?

I want your novels by tonight.

YES BOSS

Oh, and Lucas said "binman" for a joke and everybody laughed and the teacher said we mustn't make fun of binmen because without them we'd be drowning under rubbish and besides it was very well paid because of the bad smells and stuff (3,000 euros).

YO, 3,000 EUROS?

After that, everybody said, "We want to be binmen," because they thought they only worked in the mornings...

They wake up VERY EARLY, so their hours are as long as everyone else's

HEY for 3,000 euros I'd wake up early miss

And then I had an idea for a novel with a bin-girl who's also a detective because she finds clues in the rubbish, and she's the only girl in a team of men (I don't know where I get all these ideas).

BIN-GIRL
Vol 5: The Mysterious Blond

(Based on a true story told by Esther A, who is 10 years old)

Riad Sattouf

Imaginary Books

I love my dad but he's very strict: he won't let me have a smartphone and doesn't like it when I watch TV. On the other hand, he loves it when I read books. As soon as I finish one, I'm allowed to get a new one right away (no need to wait for my birthday or Christmas or whatever). We go to a bookshop where there's loads of choice and I can choose whatever I want. Now I don't know if this is the fault of the bookshop (for choosing the wrong books) or the writers (for writing bad books), but I have to say there are a lot of boring-rubbish-not-very-interesting books that I don't want to read at all. So here are a few ideas for books that, if they existed, I would want to read (LOL):

"A young girl kills herself because the girls at school make fun of her. Then she comes back to haunt them and takes her revenge on them, one by one..."
(Horror/Suspense)

THE YOUNG DEAD GIRL

The Popular Girls Club

"Some pretty, popular girls start a club to help ugly girls get over their problems and they have lots of adventures..."
(Action/Advice)

The Secret Diary of a GIRL IN LOVE

"A diary that reveals ALL the author's secrets about love..."
(Romance/Reality)

"The story of a girl who has never seen her father, only an old black-and-white photo of him, so she goes in search of the man he was..."
(Drama)

A GIRL WITH NO FATHER
ESTHER A.

Always useful, right? (Kidding)
(Guide)

500 IDEAS FOR Romantic LETTERS TO MAKE HIM love you

THE DEFINITIVE GUIDE TO DISCREET MAKE-UP

Because I love wearing make-up but I don't like it when it's too obvious!
(Techniques/Tips)

"A girl wakes up one morning and all the men on earth have disappeared! Happy days!"
(Humour)

Esther and THE WORLD WITHOUT MEN

(Based on a true story told by Esther A, who is 10 years old)

Riad Sattouf

The Crystal Ball

I got an amazing Christmas present this year. It's a crystal ball for seeing the future.

The ball answers by lighting up in different colours. "No" is blue, "maybe" is green, "ask later" is yellow...

I asked it loads of test questions like "Does my dad love me?" and "Has my older brother ever called me stupid?" where I already know the answer is "yes".

This is me discovering my destiny

Will I be beautiful one day?

You have to put batteries in it and press the top

Gasp!!! It really works!

I'm going to be beautiful!

... and "yes" is red.

Wow this is freaky!

It really KNOWS!

The ball turned red each time

My dad thought this was funny. He told me to ask it four more questions.

Will there be another world war soon?

The answer is yes

But, living in Europe, I think we'll be okay. There are 28 of us, so if another country like Russia attacks us, they'll lose. And we've got the atomic bomb to defend ourselves.

It's a bomb that destroys, like, EVERYTHING

And we've got it!

But I asked if we would win the war, just to reassure you.

See?

We're the best!

I asked it if extraterrestrials exist.

Yes they do!

But I don't think extraterrestrials are really like the ones in films. They don't really have three eyes or whatever...

They're just smaller, blue, and a bit stupid (well, not as intelligent as us anyway)

Does God exist?

HA HA HA HA!

THE TRUTH!

No!

But... How can... If God doesn't exist, then... Yo, what is this thing?

I find it really funny because all my friends believe in God, but I know he's just Father Christmas for grown-ups.

And does the Devil exist?

HA HA

(Based on a true story told by Esther A, who is 10 years old)

Riad Sattouf

The Journalist

This week, I turned eleven! Did you know that for the past year I've been telling stories about my life to a friend of my dad's who works as a cartoonist?

Yeah, I've got three boyfriends at the same time...

This is me telling him about my life

For my birthday, the cartoonist gave me the book of cartoons that he'd made from my stories.

I don't read many cartoon books. I prefer novels like "The Baby-Sitters Club"

But I liked this one because it's all about my life. And it's mostly true.

Except the boy in the train station – he kissed me on the cheek, not on my mouth

Actually those cartoons appear in a newspaper (although I can't remember its name, sorry) before they're turned into a book.

There's a journalist from that paper who'd like to interview you

Really? Sure. WHENEVER HE WANTS.

Good plan

My mum wanted us to go to a café, but I didn't want to be alone with a stranger.

So he came to our apartment

Hello

He didn't look anything like a journalist.

He looked more like a singer from the 1960s

Not VERY good-looking, but not ugly either

1960s hairstyle

But I didn't like his clothes at all.

The colours on his sweater didn't go together AT ALL

Jeans were WAY too pale

"Young and trendy" sneakers

First he said that we had to sit really far apart.

Was he scared I would eat him or what?

So is it true you like Balavoine?

Then he wanted to know if the pigeon had really been killed, if Eugenie's mum really had enormous breasts, and so on...

Yeah, it's TRUE

He asked me three times if I wasn't tired of the cartoonist calling me.

I mean, I wouldn't want him to call me every day, but...

Then, before he left, I remembered something in the book that wasn't true at all any more, so I told him.

"TANGLED" ISN'T MY FAVOURITE FILM ANY MORE.

THAT'S ALL.

(Based on a true story told by Esther A, who is 11 years old)

Riad Sattouf

The Curse

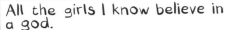

(Based on a true story told by Esther A, who is 11 years old)

Riad Sattouf

The Truth About God

My brother Antoine goes to a free (but really violent) school. Thankfully, I escaped it.

This is me with Cassandra trying to avoid Eugenie in the playground
Let's pretend we haven't seen her
Yeah

I've known Eugenie since we were little, but we haven't talked much since we started Year 6.

Oh yeah, well I think, you know...
Oh really?
Hi there!

She grew breasts and she hung around with the group of "bad boys" (the popular kids).

But when she started getting rebellious, her parents sent her to catchetizum (the school of God)
OH, Eugenie... yes?
I HAVE TO TELL YOU...

Her God-teacher, this man who wears black, put a curse on her and told her that she was going to hell unless she changed.

I said thirty "Our Fathers" every day to get the pardon, yo
IT WAS HARD, MAN

I didn't believe in God, but since all the girls I know do believe – and keep talking about him all the time – I thought, well, maybe he does exist.

I even knelt in front of the cross!

There are too many weird things in nature for them not to have been created by someone.

Who designed the orchid's petals?
Who decided the parrot's beak would look like that?
Who makes sure the patterns are the same on both the butterfly's wings?

Apparently God is a man with a white beard who controls everything (basically he knows everything, sees everything, and hears everything).

He doesn't have a wife but he does have a circle above his head
Very good looking

He watches what we do from above and he judges us to decide whether we deserve to join him in heaven when we die.

Esther's said "shit" five times this morning... How terribly vulgar... Hmm...

If we do something bad, he doesn't want us, so he sends us to hell. That's why people are scared of God. I'm scared now too.

Apparently even your eyes burn in hell
... but since you're already dead, you just keep on suffering for ever without dying again

So the priest made the sign of the cross and said "I wash away your sins, my child..."

AND IT'S LIKE HE WASHED AWAY ALL MY BELIEF IN GOD!

His breath smelled really bad, like he'd been eating poo or something...

... and I thought, "Hey, it's all a lie, he's not in contact with God cos if he was, God would say, 'Try brushing your teeth before you wash away people's sins.'"

And that's when I realized that God is just like Father Christmas, HE DOESN'T EXIST! Our parents are just making us believe in him so they can control us.

I HATE THEM!

GEE, THANKS A LOT – JUST WHEN I WAS STARTING TO BELIEVE!

(Based on a true story told by Esther A, who is 11 years old)

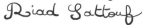

Three Lovers

My love life is strange this year. Until this week, I had three lovers at the same time but they didn't know about each other. There was the one who played basketball...

... and two who played football.

This is me in the playground in "posing" mode

My blond lover

My brown-haired lover

We never talked, we just smiled at each other lovingly

With the basketball player, it was the same — we just smiled from a distance. But then one day he smiled at me AND THEN he came to see me and started doing this "rap-style" version of a song by Oreo Sam or something, and it was crazy.

Yo, whassup? Nothing, bro! I gave it all up for the seventh art, you get the picture? Man, I'm hanging out with stars! You're in the movies, yo? Yeah I'm IN the movies...

Well, just outside, checking tickets, yo!

The lyrics were so funny! At first you think the guy in the song is a film star... but in fact he just works at a cinema!

HA HA HA HA HA HA

I laughed SOOO hard

But, you know, I only laughed. And then my two other lovers stopped playing football and started crying, each in a DIFFERENT CORNER OF THE PLAYGROUND! They couldn't stand it when they saw me laughing at Lover 1's joke!

This one hid in "I'm not crying" mode

But he was

Waaaah

And this one, well, you'd have thought the world was ending

BOTH THEIR HEARTS HAD BEEN BROKEN AT THE SAME TIME AND FOR THE SAME REASON AND THEY NEVER EVEN KNEW IT! But, you know, why did they never come and talk to me? I was right there, waiting for them.

Oh well, that's life

When I saw them crying, I decided I'd just keep the basketball player as my lover. It's tough to take right now, but it'll mean less suffering in the future.

(Based on a true story told by Esther A, who is 11 years old)

Riad Sattouf

The Club

So the reason I go to a private school, according to my beloved father, is that free schools "are shit". Just to be clear, we're not rich. At all.

This is me and him in the street (he's protecting me from the guy who always sits in front of the supermarket and scares me)

I'm fairly popular but I'm not the most popular girl in my school because I'm not interested in BRANDS.

Are those Vans... or not?

Well, I'm a little bit interested but I'm not very good at recognizing them

At the start of the year, some of the students started doing bad-boy stuff (talking about sex, swearing, dressing like rappers).

The headmaster summoned the students' parents and said they needed to discipline their children

This is him telling Lucas to pull his trousers up

You could see his boxer shorts

One of the bad boys was a girl called Lina. This is how she used to be:

Yo, whassup?

Lay it on me bro

She called everybody "bro", even other girls

The headmaster talked to her parents

Now she's normal... But she wears a new pair of shoes **EVERY DAY**.

Platform soles

"Bainmal" boots (or something)

Her sister's "Marc J Cubs" pumps

Her family is, like, super-rich.

I got them for 98 euros on sale in London

She talks to me sometimes

WOW

In other words, even on sale they're way too expensive for someone like me

She even has a pair with a real cartoon strip on them.

I really like this pair

I want them SO much

So the ex-bad boys have now started a club of people who wear white "Stan Smiss" sneakers.

Look how white their sneakers are

All you need is a pair of Stan Smiss and you can be their friend.

HI!

Hey, I love your Stan Smith Bolds

Even though he's ugly

So anyway, the other day, Lina gave me a pair of hers!

Yo, I don't wear them any more. And they're fakes

OH THANK YOU THAT'S SO KIND

They have a gold strip just here

So I put them on and went to see the members of the club.

HI THERE!

Uh sorry but you can't get in the Stan Smith team with those. They're not real, they're just cheap rip-offs

HA HA

They spotted them from ten feet away! HOW IS THAT EVEN POSSIBLE?

(Based on a true story told by Esther A, who is 11 years old)

Riad Sattouf

The Lost Soul

I would say I have a "super-sensitive" personality.

I feel other people's pain. I'm really good at seeing things through their eyes. And it's hard sometimes.

I realized that he was incapable of love. I'd thought he was in love with me but really he was just pretending. It gave me a shock.

Well, I think he believed that his feelings were sincere. We went out together for THREE days. On the first day, a girl came up to me and SLAPPED ME! She was his ex-girlfriend, the one he'd dumped for me. That should have set off alarm bells.

I didn't even realize that, when I thought I was his girlfriend, I was really just playing Cupid for him and Lina! They got married on the afternoon of the day he dumped me.

I wanted to kill her, but then he dumped her for an older girl with a long ponytail... He's got a serious problem. He'll be very unhappy in life if he just goes from girl to girl and never feels anything.

Despite his passion for basketball and his amazing looks (the dark, mysterious type), I have a feeling that life is going to be hard for him.

I really don't know what we can do to help him.

(Based on a true story told by Esther A, who is 11 years old)

82

Reproduction

I have a secret love. His name is Mathis.

This is me gazing tenderly at him

He loves me too

He should have been a delegate but he was cheated of victory

This week, we started learning about "human reproduction", which is basically how babies are "made" in women's bellies.

I've made some reproduction flash cards and we'll go through them together

No, it's not badly drawn: my teacher really is a dwarf or something

---

Before, I used to think that people made babies by hugging.

My parents do a lot of hugging

One day in summer camp, a boy hugged me because we'd won at dodgeball...

YEEAAAH!

That night, I cried because I felt sure I was going to have a baby (I had stomach ache too).

Esther! What's the...

SOORRRY DAAAD I MADE A BABY IN CAAMP!

WAAA

But then I found out how babies were really made by watching YouPorn on Eugenie's phone.

I lied last year when I said I didn't go on that site

In fact I did and it was horrible

It shouldn't be allowed

It's this website that shows videos where people make babies by being violent or whatever.

Afterwards we didn't talk because we were so traumatized

And that's the truth

So anyway, the teacher started telling us about reproduction and all that but WITHOUT telling us how it was "done"! WEIRD, RIGHT?

So... Once the man and the woman have... you know... um, well, we're going to study what happens after that

Lots of us didn't know at all

Someone asked how it was "done" and some other people laughed. The teacher told us, "If you want a detailed description, ask your parents". And then Kalila said:

Miss, can I leave the class? It's not right to talk about these things

---

The teacher said "No" and asked if anybody knew what the ovum and spermatozoa were.

Kalila put her hands over her ears (I think it's her God who won't let her discuss this stuff)

Lucas, the class delegate, asked if he was allowed to reply even if the answer was shocking. The teacher said "yes".

The ovum is the girls' egg and the spermatozoa are the little creatures inside men's sperm

Sperm is made in the balls

Everybody started laughing and talking and the teacher told us to calm down. And just then, my lover Mathis turned to me and whispered:

Esther! I've got sperm, you know...

He was, like, bright red

And I was like "?!?!?!?!?!?!?!?!?!"

(Based on a true story told by Esther A, who is 11 years old)

Riad Sattouf

Single

So last week we started studying human reproduction.

This is me when Mathis (my secret love) told me he had "sperm"

Umm...

Thankfully the teacher told us all to stop talking, because I had no idea what to say (definitely not age-appropriate).

("Sperm" is like a boy's period, and there are spermatozoa inside it)

So the teacher told us what happened between the spermatozoa and the ovum and all that.

Well... Okay. Let's start

The fertilization of the ovum

Yep, she was embarrassed

In fact, it's really just like life, this whole thing with the spermatozoa and the ovum.

The spermatozoa are the boys...

... and the ovum is the girl

There are billions of spermatozoa swimming as fast as they can into the girl's belly to find the ovum (yep, there's only one ovum).

Quiiick

Where is it?

Psst! Ovum!

And they all fight to be the first one to get there (not surprising – they're boys). And the ovum chooses just one of them to marry (I think she swallows it or something)...

YOU! COME ON!

Argh!

Noooo! Why him, yo?

Fuck, no!

YES

GET IN THERE

Once the ovum has swallowed the spermatozoon she chose, all the others die miserably.

Yep, billions of spermatozoa die all alone each time this happens

Ungh

Then the ovum and her husband go to the Youterrace, which is like an apartment or something inside the woman's belly, and they stay there for nine months.

And that makes a baby which is like a mix of the two parents.

Just an "example"

If the ovum stays alone and no spermatozoa come to see her, well, she dies too in a river of blood.

Uunngh

So being single guarantees you a miserable death

The death of the ovum is called the "period".

Lina, in my class, has had her period, but only once

It's called the "monarch" or something.

Will I have that too? Ugh!

I hate all these subjects (body – sex – how babies are made, etc.)

I think it's WRONG that we're forced to learn all that when we're not interested!

(Based on a true story told by Esther A, who is 11 years old)

Riad Sattouf

Making Babies

Panel 1:
I'm so sick of all this stuff about reproduction.

"This is me writing the word 'reproduction'" →

Our PETITE (that's the right word) teacher →

Panel 2:
Esther, write it here! You've still got space at the bottom!

Panel 3:
AHWHAHAHA HAHAHA HAH
SPACE AT THE BOTTOM HA HA HAHA
HAHA HA HAHA BOTTOM

Panel 4:
All boys are obsessed with sex. It's literally all they think about.

Even Arthur, who's usually oblivious, is just like the others →

BHAHAHA BOTTOM HEE HEE HEE

Panel 5:
The only girl I know who's like that is Louisa, a friend from my dance class. Last year, I invited her to my birthday party and she did this.

Oh Ken Oh yesss harder

Stop it! What's wrong with you?

Ken from Ken and Barbie

She's obsessed

Panel 6:
I mean, us girls are also interested in love and all that, but only because of the babies we'll have.

I'm going to have a baby on my 13th birthday

OH REALLY?

Well yeah, why wait?

Panel 7:
Cassandra wants a baby too, but she's the opposite of Louisa.

I do want a baby but not until I'm retired.

I want to enjoy life before then.

Panel 8:
I dream of having children, but I'd prefer to get them without having sex or giving birth.

Eugenie told me once that her sister and her sister's boyfriend slept together and she'd heard her sister moaning in pain and the next morning her sister had told her, "Don't worry, we were just having sex"

I was shocked

Panel 9:
Birth is horrible because apparently they give you an injection to take away the pain, and the injection is ten times more painful than giving birth.

Don't move! This may hurt a bit

AGH!

SKWIRT

They stab you in the back!

Panel 10:
I'm still pretty young, though, so maybe they'll come up with a way to make babies remotely in the future?

She looks just like me!

ROBOWOMB 50

And my belly will stay flat (yesss!)

Panel 11:
I saw a cartoon once of a white swan that was vomiting babies out of its beak to give them to women or something.

Whose is this?

Mine! Mine!

Panel 12:
Sorry, I meant a stork, not a swan! Why did I say a swan?!

This was a really good idea →

Why isn't life like that?

(Based on a true story told by Esther A, who is 11 years old)

Riad Sattouf

The Outing

Last Saturday, Cassandra came to our apartment like she does almost every Saturday.

This is me kissing her on the cheek to say hello

Okay, girls, Marie-Pierre and I have discussed this and we've decided to let you walk around the neighbourhood ON YOUR OWN...

... and here's 5 euros to spend on whatever you want!

It was the first time in my life I'd been allowed out without a grown-up!

We dressed in "sunny day" mode and went out into the street!

(Yep, Cassandra got her hair straightened)

Flower t-shirt

I love these red heart sunglasses, they're really FUN.

They're not a famous brand or anything, just plastic, but they're still cool

The first thing we did was go to the bakery and look at mini-donuts.

5 euros divided by 60 centimes... how many can we get?

HMM!

We bought 8 filled with Nutella (like a really yummy chocolate cream)!

My mum hardly ever gets me donuts, and never more than one

We ate them all and watched the video of "Friend Zone" by Matty B on Cassandra's phone.

We sat on the bench like this

In "do what we want" mode

Matty B is a kid rapper who's really good-looking (like a young Justin Bieber) who made a video where he loves a girl but she thinks of him as just a friend (very funny).

I think we could be

Something like more than just friends

Afterwards we talked about how we might bump into him in the street (yeah, right)!

♪ Mattyyy we're here where are you? ♪ We want to be more than just friends!

Crying with laughter

I yelled that

And then I saw a boy who looked just like him (he was with a Renoi).

They didn't know I was looking at them, because of my glasses

Foot-baller hair

We were only allowed out for one hour, so we went home and I said to my mum:

Yo, Mum! Can we go out again next week for 2 hours with 20 euros?

Thanks

Her: "..."

So that was my first outing!

(Based on a true story told by Esther A, who is 11 years old)

Riad Sattouf

86

The Nice Boy

Do you prefer girls or boys? I DEFINITELY prefer girls. We would be perfectly fine without any boys at all. All we need them for is making babies. That's the only useful thing they do. I've had boyfriends of course. But, to be honest, I only loved them for their good looks or their smiles. As soon as we started talking, it was... how can I put this? Just a load of crap, basically. They only like boring things, they're always swearing, and they're way too full of themselves. I have an older brother called Antoine and he's so, sooo stupid. For example, when we sit next to each other on the sofa, if I accidentally touch him, he'll say "Get off me, I'm going to puke!" Isn't that just really stupid and annoying? And, as if that wasn't enough, four months ago, I got ANOTHER brother. But I have to admit, he has changed the way I think about boys a little bit. The other day, my mum was about to take a shower and she put him in my arms and I held him like that. I looked at him and — for the first time ever — he SMILED at me!

OMG HE'S SOOOOOO CUTE!

(Based on a true story told by Esther A, who is 11 years old)

Riad Sattouf

Passion

I always liked bags, but now I think I'm starting to develop a passion for them.

This is me with my old "Frozen" schoolbag

I got it in Year 2

I really loved it because I loved the film (I still like it now even if it seems kind of "little-kiddish"), but I don't use it anymore.

Back then I totally identified with Elsa and Anna, the sisters in the kingdom of Arendelle

But now it's over (that's life)

I also had a "Violetta" bag that I don't use any more (I don't watch that show now... well, I do sometimes, but I don't like it as much as I used to).

Nobody has this at my school now

I really liked that character though

Now I have a simple cloth bag with a flower pattern. It goes well with anything (very practical).

Ideal for shopping with my mum on sunny days

In fact, I like anything that can "contain" stuff or "carry" stuff.

My old "pink shark" pencil case. A bit babyish but I like it

I used to be crazy about it

Today, this is more my style:

Graffiti-style writing (graffiti is street art that people paint on walls in cities and I love it)

Everything "real" comes from the street ("real" as in "keeping it real, yo")

In recent years, I've had this pink-and-green "flower" backpack. Since my parents don't have much money, and I don't want to be a burden on them, I kept it all the way through Year 4 AND Year 5.

It's nice, but the colours are a bit "little girl"

Me, striking a pose (LOL)

But anyway, this year I got sick of it. In fact, Lina – this girl in my class who has a passion for fashion and is very rich (she has a pair of new shoes almost every day) – said this to me:

Aren't you sick of that flowery bag? You should get an Eastpak like me. They're not expensive and they're really solid...

Everybody at school has an Eastpak and they're really good, but I always thought they were too expensive. So I asked my dad if I could have one.

Abso FFFF lute FFFF ly FFFF not FFFF

My dad does a lot of exercise

But in the end we went to Go Sport and my dad bought one for me (he can't resist me).

50 euros is expensive! I expect you to keep it ALL the way through secondary school...

I PROMISE, DAD!

Plastic-wrapped

But then I put it on at home and the straps were, like, really stiff, and I started crying.

The horror!

I thought it was broken

It's fiiiine! It's just because it's empty and new... Put a dumbbell inside, you'll see...

I did what he said and it was perfect!

My dad, the man who solves all my problems

I LOVE HIM SOOOO MUCH

(Based on a true story told by Esther A, who is 11 years old)

Riad Sattouf

Death

I'm going to tell you how I got the biggest fright of my life and how I ended up with 120 euros because of it.

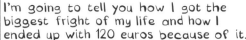

This is me in "pose" mode

My brother Antoine

I don't want to be a vampire!

It was last week. We'd stayed at home and my brother was being weirdly nice.

Chica vaaampiro chica Vam Vam Vaaaddm

He'd agreed to watch "Chica Vampiro", a TV series I love

Our parents were in the park with Gaëtan. Suddenly there was a knock at the door.

BANG! BANG! BANG!

Dad told us not to open it

Did... did you lock it?

No... Did you?

EEE... KLAK!

The door opened!

And someone came in!

DAAAAD?

Footsteps

TAP
TAP
TAP
TAP

YO, I'M DEATH

My brother jumped up to protect me!

AAAAAAHARRRRRGGGHHH

SO THE KILLER STABBED HIM!

AAAAAARRRRRGGGGHHH

CHAKK
CHAKK
CHAKK

I screamed at the top of my voice and I turned around and saw Lucien, my brother's friend, take off his mask. And my brother stood up and said:

AAAAAARRRRRGGGGHHH

Es... Esther we were just kidding...

Fuck, man, why's she screaming like that?

Afterwards I felt sick. I couldn't breathe and Lucien ran out in tears because he thought he'd killed me.

Esther... Please breathe! I thought it'd make you laugh... Please don't tell Dad — I'll give you all my savings!

HH
HH

And suddenly I felt a bit better.

Okay... Give me the money.

I will! Right away...

When my dad came home, I told him what had happened and he said, "Keep the money" and he got really mad at Antoine!

He wanted to report Antoine to the police (LOL)

Antoine cried

My 120 euros

I told you he was stupid

(Based on a true story told by Esther A, who is 11 years old)

Riad Sattouf

Lezzer

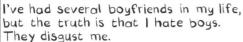

I've had several boyfriends in my life, but the truth is that I hate boys. They disgust me.

This is me in the playground watching them, a few months ago ←

The worst boys are the ones who are "girly": they're just like girls, but they're actually boys. I mean, what's the point? I prefer girls.

For example, Mitchell's in Year 6 and at break time he plays with some Year 3 girls (yep, you read that right)!

When another boy calls him a "queer" (that means gay), sometimes he just bursts out crying.

HA HA look at that queer!

WAAAH SNNFF WAAAH

What does "queer" mean?

Fight him, instead of just whining like a girl!

And then there are those really boring boys who just "don't exist". They're not good-looking or ugly, they play football and they swear a lot, but nobody cares about them.

Him, for example

I'm going to fucking cross it!

JUST FUCKING PASS IT

I didn't tell you this, but once, one of those boys fell off a wall and some guys came with an ambulance to take him away.

Move your legs, lad! Don't fall asleep, lad! You hear me? Lad?

I think he might have broken his neck or something...

But at lunchtime, his "friends" just played football as usual, like nothing had happened. They couldn't care less about him!

I wonder if it's almost worse to be that kind of boy than to be like Mitchell

GOOOOAAAALLLL

FUCKING GET IN!

(He did get better BTW)

And then there are the bad boys. They're really popular and they only talk about two things: sex and fighting. They're horrible.

An' he wer' like "Fuck yer MOTHER you son of a bitch" an' I said "Whatcha say to me you fucking queer?" an' so anyway I smashed that motherfucking son of a bitch in his fucking mouth

Louis, an ex-boyfriend of mine from Year 5 →

Sorry for all the swear words but that's the reality of my life

They're really tough. For example, one day Lucas fell over while playing football and injured his face.

Fucking excellent

I FUCKED UP my face, man HA HA!

He didn't cry at all even though he was pouring with blood (I must admit that impressed me a bit. It's, like, superhuman or something)

The other day, when we were talking about how crap boys are, Cassandra (my best friend) said:

You really hate boys, don't you? Maybe you're a lezzer?

"Lezzer" means "gay woman"

My dad has a female cousin who's gay. One day she came to my granny's house with two of her lesbian friends.

Good journey?

God, the traffic jams...

Hello Esther

Honestly, they looked just like men. They really copied their style. What's the point in not loving men if you're just going to look like them?

If I was gay, I'd be super-feminine and I'd only love very very very feminine women (that's just my opinion, sorry if you're offended)

Yo, whas-sup?

She said that even though she's, like, 40 years old!

So I don't like boys, I don't like gay women... I'm going to be single for the rest of my life.

I love Lucas. I was so scared for him when he fell... and he just laughed!

The good news is that I won't be the only one, I think...

(Based on a true story told by Esther A, who is 11 years old)

Riad Sattouf

The Attack

My name is Esther, I'm 11 years old and I'm sooo scared. My best friend Cassandra told me that there'd been a terrorist attack in Belgium. She said that actually everybody knew this guy was a terrorist, even the police, but nobody did anything. She said he should really have been in prison but instead he was just free to go wherever he wanted. And then he told the police where he was going and he put the bomb in the metro and it killed loads of people. And Cassandra told me she saw a TV programme that said there were thousands of people just like him all over Europe and that nobody could do anything about it and that it was going to happen again. And then she cried.

My dad tries so hard to protect me that it's probably better if I don't ask him stuff any more. Because I can tell it stresses him out to have to lie to me to protect me (and then I get stressed out by seeing him stressed out by having to lie, etc. etc.)

(Based on a true story told by Esther A, who is 11 years old)

Riad Sattouf

The Test

The good thing about time passing too slowly is that it does pass in the end: the school year is almost over.

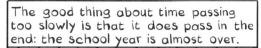

This is me and Cassandra complaining about the atmosphere at our school

God it's SO boring here

Tell me about it!

We were supposed to go to the same private secondary school next year (Cassandra is very poor but her mum sweats blood to give her a better life) and we were happy about that.

Can't wait till we get out of here...

I know!

But then one evening my beloved father came into my bedroom and this is what he told me:

Esther... We've got less money now that Gaëtan is with us... I'm not going to be able to pay for private school any more... You'll have to go to the public school...

in SHOCK

My world collapsed. We'd become even poorer than Cassandra!

I was so sad that I cried my eyes out (it's an expression: my eyes didn't actually pour out of my head)

I don't know what it's like where you live, but in Paris if you want to go to a free school you don't get to choose it — you just have to go to the one closest to your home.

And the one closest to us is really horrible. That's where my brother goes

My brother goes to a ZPEP, which is the official name for a crappy school. It's a dangerous place with loads of violence.

In primary school, my brother was like this:

Hair cut by my mum →

← Almost cute

Not too stupid →

Liked LEGO

Wanted to be an astronaut

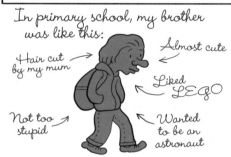

Now he's in a ZPEP:

Wants footballer hair →

Really stupid all the time

Go fuck yer fat ho grandma's pussy yo

Says a thousand terrible swear words per minute

Wants to be a rapper

Since I'm a good student, my dad signed me up to take a test. If I pass it, I'll get to go to a much better school in the centre of Paris!

It'll be hard, but you can do it! You have to try!

These schools are in neighbourhoods so expensive that only billionaires can afford to live there, and most of the students are from rich families. They sometimes let in people from other places, but it's really hard. There's an exam and an interview.

It was near the Seine

My dad wasn't allowed to go in.

Be yourself and you'll be fine!

I felt like I was leaving him for ever

I'd never seen such a massive school before. It was like a castle. I got lost. So I went over to this woman who was standing in the courtyard. She was reading a piece of paper. There was nobody else around.

H... Hello... I... I've come to take the entrance exam and... and I don't know where to go...

Oh really? That's lucky — I've come to take the test too! It's Door B3...

Are you telling me this girl is my age?

(Based on a true story told by Esther A, who is 11 years old)

Riad Sattouf

92

Heinrich

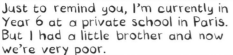

Just to remind you, I'm currently in Year 6 at a private school in Paris. But I had a little brother and now we're very poor.

This is me listening to my dad tell me that I'll have to go to a free school next year

I had two choices: go to the same school as my brother Antoine, which is near where we live but is a ZPEP (that's a school with loads of violence)...

Esther I don't want to scare you or anything, but little white Babtous like you get blown away at my school, yo!

BLOWN UH-WAAAY!

KLIK KLIK

This is him telling me

Hee hee

What a jerk →

... or try to get into a very posh free school in the centre of Paris by passing a test that's supposed to be super-difficult...

Which is what I did

The guy next to me was Portuguese or some-thing

There were about 20 of us in one big room

No, this girl isn't my age — she's trying to get into Year 10

A man in a suit came in and gave us some papers. There was a short text with a few questions.

Year 7? Here...

I... Yes, I...

I was in "I'm going to fail" mode. I was trembling

The text told the story of a young couple who move to a different neighbourhood, but their dog Heinrich doesn't want to leave so it runs away from them and stays in the neighbourhood.

It was a Yorkshire terrier and apparently it was a bit full of itself

(I hate dogs. I prefer cats)

Then I read the questions and I couldn't believe how easy they were.

QUESTIONS
1) Is the couple elderly?
2) What is the dog's name?
3) What breed is it?
4) Does the dog want to move?
5) Imagine the rest of the story (two pages maximum) ....

I answered the questions and started to write the rest of the story as it came to me...

I want to be an editor when I grow up, so it was easy for me →

Skrtch Skrtch

"Heinrich wanders around the neighbourhood. He's all alone. His owners have left. He's proud of himself."

I want to stay here. I can manage without them

"He doesn't know that eyes are observing him through a window."

"Night falls and he starts to feel hungry. Just then, he hears a soft voice calling him."

Oh, little lost doggie! Little doggie, are you hungry?

"Heinrich turns and sees a very beautiful young woman dressed in black. She smiles at him. She's holding a leg of smoked ham."

Come and taste this lovely ham, little doggie!

"Starving, Heinrich starts devouring the ham. 'What a great idea it was to stay here,' he thinks. The young woman tenderly pets him."

I love dogs! I'm going to call you Antoine after my brother... Eat! Eat more...

"But Heinrich's head is spinning... He's falling asleep..."

"When he opens his eyes, he's in a small cage in a basement. The sweet young woman's expression has changed. Her face is cold and harsh now. 'What's happening?' Heinrich wonders. 'I miss my owners. I should have gone with them...'"

Ah, awake at last, **ANTOINE**! I'd like to try a little experiment, just the two of us...

(Based on a true story told by Esther A, who is 11 years old)

Riad Sattouf

The Pipe-Cleaner Woman

Okay, so I'm going to continue with my story. I had two pages LMFAO (that's a rude way of saying LOL, in case you didn't know).

Me during the test, writing the rest of the story about Heinrich, an arrogant little dog who abandoned his owners

He is now the prisoner of the crazy young woman in black, who decides to punish him in the place of her hated dead brother...

BEG ME TO FORGIVE YOU FOR WHAT YOU DID TO ME, ANTOINE! OR I'LL SKIN YOU ALIVE!

Completely nuts

?

Weird horror — I love it

In the end, the woman is arrested and locked up and the dog is saved and returned to his former masters (although he now has only one ear because the crazy woman cut off the other one).

And so, the arrogant little dog learned his lesson

(I really hate dogs)

The boy next to me finished very quickly, and afterwards he dropped his phone twice. The third time he did it, the man in the suit who gave us the papers confiscated the phone and said:

Are you aware of where you are? And what you're doing here?

Hey it's not my fault

Afterwards they picked up our papers and we went into a big, dingy room where we had to wait to be interviewed.

The ceiling was crumbling — look!

Mouldy

An hour later, a very nice (but extremely ugly) woman showed me into her office and asked me to read the story of the dog out loud.

"Heinrich the dog heard his masters calling him. But he didn't care: 'No, I'm not going to leave this neighbourhood,' he thought in his canine cerebellum"...

Body shaped like a pipe-cleaner

Then she asked me why I wanted to go to this school rather than the one near our home. I didn't dare tell her that we'd become poor since the birth of my little brother and that I didn't want to go to a ZPEP like my other brother because it had turned him into a moron.

Actually, um... well, basically your school is very famous and posh, so...

She didn't say anything. She wrote something down. Then she asked me what I wanted to do when I was older.

I want to be an editor of YA novels.

A writer?

No, editor.

Editor.

I want to... I'd really like to choose books based on my tastes and publish them. The writers would ask me to read them and I'd say, "It's good but put some more romance here, or more action there..." and so they'd end up being my books too, because I love reading. I read a lot.

She wrote something down. She asked me if I had a mobile phone. I said my dad wouldn't let me have one. And she said:

Good. He's quite right.

So the pipe-cleaner woman is ugly AND boring

And then something really weird happened. She put away her things, smiled, and said:

Tell me about your parents... What do they do?

The interview is over...

I almost lied and told her they did super-cool jobs (artist, fashion designer, etc.) but in the end I said, "My dad's a trainer at a gym and my mum works in insurance" (the truth, basically).

And who do you prefer — your father or your mother?

(Based on a true story told by Esther A, who is 11 years old)

The Trap

So this is me answering some very personal questions about my family, asked by an extremely ugly woman who decides which students get into this super-posh free school and which don't

She'd told me the interview was over, she'd closed her folder, and then she'd carried on asking me questions!

You don't have any preference at all between your father and your mother?

Well, no!

Hmm...

Are they married?

I... um... yes...

Do they sometimes stop you doing things?

Well yeah, like everybody

"Like everybody?"

Like all parents...

What don't they let you do, for example?

I dunno, go out alone at night...

REALLY?

Well yeah... I mean, I'm only 11

11 isn't that young. Surely you can go out with your friends in the evening?

Well, no... I don't know...

I thought it was really weird that she was saying that. I realized she was trying to trap me into telling her the truth and that really stressed me out. I wanted to cry.

She was using a lie as bait to catch the truth

Do your parents tell you off sometimes?

You... you told me it was over...

Why did I say that?

When she opened the folder and wrote something down, I knew I'd blown it

You'll receive our response to your application by post at your address in the 6th arrondissement.

That is where you live, correct?

Did someone love this woman?

Yes, we've just moved.

My dad told me to say this! We actually live in the 17th arrondissement. My mum used her work address, which is close to the posh school, as her personal address, so that I could take the test...

I cried sooooooo much when I saw my dad again...

DAAAD I'M SO SORRY I FAAAIIILED

I totally blew it

... AND YET, INCREDIBLE BUT TRUE, I WAS ACCEPTED!

My dad was so happy that I thought he was going to cry

This is the greatest day of my life

Making my dad happy is my favourite thing in the world

(Based on a true story told by Esther A, who is 11 years old)

Riad Sattouf

95

The List

I really like lists. I think they're very revealing about the person who makes them.

This is me making a list of things I find BEAUTIFUL

---

1. My dad's profile, backlit by the sun.

He looks like a god or a film star or something

---

2. The irises of my dad's eyes seen very close-up.

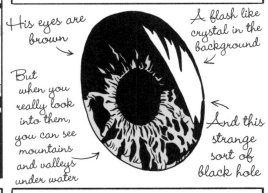

His eyes are brown

But when you really look into them, you can see mountains and valleys under water

A flash like crystal in the background

And this strange sort of black hole

---

3. The thickness of my baby brother's hair.

The exact colour of gold

Like, obscenely thick

He's only 8 months old and has no idea how lucky he is

---

4. Blue (the colour).

Joke photo taken on holiday

Me dressed all in blue in front of a blue sky

Like, whoa!

I look almost invisible

---

5. The aurora borealis (I've never seen it but apparently it's incredible).

If you don't know what it is, you can see it in the background of the poster for "Frozen" (an excellent Disney film)

It's this bit

---

6. Gold (the metal and the colour).

My mum's jewellery box (which used to be my grand-mother's)

Me trying on my mum's gold necklace (a bit too shiny)

I prefer matte gold

---

7. A woman in good make-up.

Do you recognize her? Yes, it's my mum!

The power of make-up, huh?!

---

8. All the different models of iPhones.

They're like useful jewellery

But I'm not allowed to have one

This is my dad's

---

9. The stars of "Chica Vampiro", a new comedy series about vampires that I really like.

Santiago Talledo

Greeicy Rendón

---

10. Modesty aside, I think I look very nice from behind.

My dad took this photo during our most recent holiday

HA HA!

JUST KIDDING!

(Based on a true story told by Esther A, who is 11 years old)

Riad Sattouf

The Beach

During our last holiday, we went to visit my grandmother in Bain-de-Bretagne (a town in Brittany with a strange name). It was good. One afternoon, we went for a walk on the beach in Saint-Malo (it's a really beautiful beach but there are too many dogs off the lead and that scares me). We were walking and I was thinking about how I'll soon have braces on my teeth and I was worrying that it would make me ugly, etc. (you know, dark thoughts), when suddenly something really weird happened.

She disappeared towards the horizon and afterwards I wasn't scared of my braces any more or of getting old! I SAW MYSELF IN THE FUTURE AND REALLY LIKED WHAT I SAW!

(Based on a true story told by Esther A, who is 11 years old)

Riad Sattouf

The Improv Club

I adore my mum, even though we're very different.

This is me thinking that she's put on weight since my brother was born

My parents met when they were teenagers and they've been together ever since.

There's a photo of them looking really young on the fridge

The main thing I have in common with my mum is that we both adore my dad.

And how are my favourite ladies in the world this morning?

MWAH

He said "ladies", plural. I love him

Apart from that, she's much more "straight" than I am. Like, she works for a company that does "insurance" or something...

Our "premium serenity" contract covers ALL risks for your place of residence.

It sounds good!

It is good.

She says stuff like this all day long

Insurance is this thing that "protects"... For example, if there's a fire in your apartment, the insurance company pays you back for everything that's been destroyed. But in reality, before paying out, they try to find as many reasons as they can NOT to pay (like trying to prove you started the fire yourself – sneaky, huh?).

I'm sorry but we can't reimburse you. The "multi-risk" contract doesn't cover that risk.

How can she do that as a job? It's a mystery to me.

I'm more interested in "artistic" stuff than my mum is. She has no curiosity about music, for example.

I've already planned the names of our kids, our wedding date, I've already planned the classy ceremony on the beach, I'll drive an R8 and she can drive a Mini, we'll live on the 5th floor of a beautiful apartment near the Seine...

TURN THAT CRAP DOWN!

Première fois" by Soub (I love this song)

My mum claims she's a bit artistic because she does "improv theatre". That means, like, sketches that you make up as you go along (good idea).

Next challenge: MIME!

Sometimes we go and see her at the club

The actors are given a subject and they have to invent a story.

The theme of the mime is "The beach!" Let's have a round of applause!

For example, my mum is pretending to arrive at the beach with her bag...

She sways her hips (to show she's playing a flirty, frivolous woman)

She's not at all like that when she goes to the beach

Then she mimes spreading out her towel.

I adore my mum, but honestly she's really bad at this

Anyone could do better if they really tried

Moving her hands much too quickly

It makes me ashamed to see her doing this stuff. My dad, on the other hand, thinks she's fantastic (good thing too, given they've been together for 20 years).

I wish I could teleport away from here

HA HA HA!

Here's a funny question: if my dad had been given the choice between my mum and me at the same age, who would he have chosen?

This is her pretending to read a crappy magazine on the beach

(Based on a true story told by Esther A, who is 11 years old)

Riad Sattouf

34 Years

My life has been horrible recently because I had two enormous zits...

This is me looking in the mirror and feeling totally depressed

... They were right next to each other ON MY NOSE.

Not only was this extremely ugly (and disgusting) but it really hurt too.

The pain woke me up at night and it felt like this → TAK TAK

I'd had small zits before but nothing like this.

They were smaller, on my forehead, and they didn't hurt at all

—Hi...
—You look beautiful
—Thank you. You look beautifuller! I mean not fuller, you don't look fuller, but more beautiful
—Thank you

From "Frozen" (masterpiece)

I tried various "old wives' remedies" (like, secret tricks) to get rid of them.

Alcohol (nope)

Clay (useless)

Lemon juice (doesn't even burn)

Toothpaste (excellent if you want your nose to smell minty)

Apart from that, useless

I'm the ONLY ONE in my school to have zits like that. None of the boys have them.

You're pretty, yo... without zits!

HA HA

Lucas, the most popular boy in school

They got bigger and bigger so my mum took me to the pharmacist, who had a foreign accent.

Oooh! Well, whatairver you do, don't burst thairm or you'll gairt scars! Heair, try this cream, it hairlps if you use it for 34 yeairs...

You hairve to put it on airvery day and wash your hands airfter...

I HAVE TO PUT IT ON FOR 34 YEARS?

I tried to hold them back but tears welled in my eyes. I couldn't believe I'd have to use that cream for 34 years!

I said, "FOR DIRTY PORES, YAIRSS?" Sorry for my axcairnt!

Then my mum and the ugly foreign pharmacist laughed at me. But there was nothing funny about it. I just felt stupid now, as well as having two massive painful zits on my nose.

HA HA!

EXCAIRLAIRNT HA HA!

OSCILLO

I put the cream on and of course it didn't work. So I squeezed the zits and all this pus squirted out (gross, but that's life) and now it's better.

In 34 years, I'll be 45 years old (!)

(Based on a true story told by Esther A, who is 11 years old)

Riad Sattouf

The Blow-up

So, this weekend, my mum and I had this huge blow-up. I get on pretty well with her, but we both have strong personalities... Anyway, we all have a body, right? And we should be able to do what we want with it, right? And nobody else should get to choose what we look like, right? You agree, right? Okay, so this has been going on for years, but I finally put a stop to it. Let me explain: on Saturday evening, my mum came into my bedroom and said, as she usually does: "Your fringe is getting long, I'm going to cut it." I looked her and I said: "You're not cutting anything! I don't want a fringe any more, okay? And would you please knock before you come in my room from now on? Thank you." She didn't say anything. You should have seen the look on her face! She was shocked! But, I mean, I don't go into her room and cut her hair, do I? Right?

After that, I gave myself the hairstyle I've wanted for years (but my mum wouldn't let me have)

Looks different, right?

I stuck the short hair from my fringe under the long hair, which I swept forward

I can almost do this kind of pose now

Needs to get a bit longer first

Stylish, right?

(I've got two huge zit scars on my nose — don't look, they're horrible)

How could I have walked round with a fringe all this time?

And I can still have a ponytail if I want — with a fresh twist

And when I'm in "antisocial" mode, I can put it like this so I don't see anyone

And it hides my zits too (except on my nose, sigh)

What will the kids at school think when they see me on Monday?

Hey, Esther's got rid of her fringe!

Wow, she's really changed lately

Yeah, she looks cool, yo

And if I sweep my hair back like this and put on make-up, I look really grown-up, don't you think?

(Based on a true story told by Esther A, who is 11 years old)

Riad Sattouf

Left and Right

If someone asked me, I'd say I was on the right.

This is me and my new hairstyle arriving at school →

Actually, I don't know anything about politics.

What will people think? (Not that I care, really)

In France, if you're on the right, it means that you're, like, in favour of people travelling, discovering the world, coming to live in our country and all that.

Ohh you're SO BEAUTIFUL

You really like it?

My best friend Cassandra →

The right is... loving other people, even if they're not like us (like they don't have the same tastes or interests or whatever).

You look like a model on TV!

She changed her hair too, not long ago →

Our mini-teacher (she's small so I call her mini-teacher — funny, right?) is on the right. She's obsessed by poverty and she's always telling us that we should "retribute wealth" or something.

Can anyone give me a definition of sustainable development?

I'm interested in the same things she is →

We're both on the right →

Being on the left is, like, the opposite. It's saying, "This is our country, go away," or, "This is mine, hands off!" to people in need (I just don't understand that kind of attitude).

Mathis, my secret love →

Développement durable

Being on the left is... what's the name of that woman who's always like, "Yeah Africans go back to Africa" etc.?

She's blonde and she's got really small teeth... and she doesn't like Rebeus (Arab people) or Renois (Black people). I'm the opposite — I think we should all mix together, like one big happy family!

YOUR NEW HARECUT TURNS ME ON ♡

LOLLLLL

But I don't know why everybody talks about "left" and "right". I heard on the TV that François Hollande was on the right (some protesters said that).

Hee hee Ha ha   What's so funny?

Why are you laughing?

We're laughing at Esther and her new hairstyle, miss!

PFFF

SHE LOOKS LIKE RAPUNZEL, YO

My ex-friend Eugenie

I wanted to say to the teacher, you're supposed to be on the right, but laughing at other people's appearance is cruel and it's what people on the left do.

Come on now, calm down Esther's hairstyle is very pretty

HA HA HA   HA HA   HAHAHA

Rapunzel   Me

What do you think?

(Based on a true story told by Esther A, who is 11 years old)

101

Body Language

I have two brothers: Antoine, who's 15 years old (and I hate him because he's an idiot) and Gaëtan, who's 9 months old (and I adore him, for now).

I wonder if there are any jobs where you get paid for observing babies and noting down your observations? I'd be pretty good at a job like that, I think.

At school, the teacher told us "We're not DESCENDED from monkeys, we ARE a type of monkey." Well, my brother is also a type of worm.

This is me in "experimenting on my baby brother" mode

Hff Gaah

I like testing how bendy he is

He's happy

The splits? No problem!

GOO

He just wriggles and rolls around

I'm really proud that I can do all the things he can do (which means bendiness is in our genes).

I enjoy this "physical and dynamic" dialogue that I have with him. It goes beyond language.

Actually I think he's fascinated by me (well, that's normal – I am his big sister).

I'm naturally supple

Well, I am a dancer (I go to dance class)

He watches me closely

Look how cute he is when he watches me roll across the floor

He can sit up and follow me with his eyes now.

What's funny is the emotions you can provoke in him, like, really easily.

If I move like this, he gets all stressed (LOL)

Hi there!   Hi there!

I give a big smile

He smiles

Then suddenly I glare at him

?

GRRR

And then I smile...

Waaah

And he laughs while crying!

BOOO!

My mum doesn't really "kiffe" my experiments (for us young people, "kiffe" means, like, being really into something).

(Based on a true story told by Esther A, who is 11 years old)

Riad Sattouf

The Mummy Dog

The other night I had a dream about a giant mummy dog and her little puppies (whereas I HATE dogs in real life). Weirdly, I was asleep in my dream! I mean, I knew I was asleep.

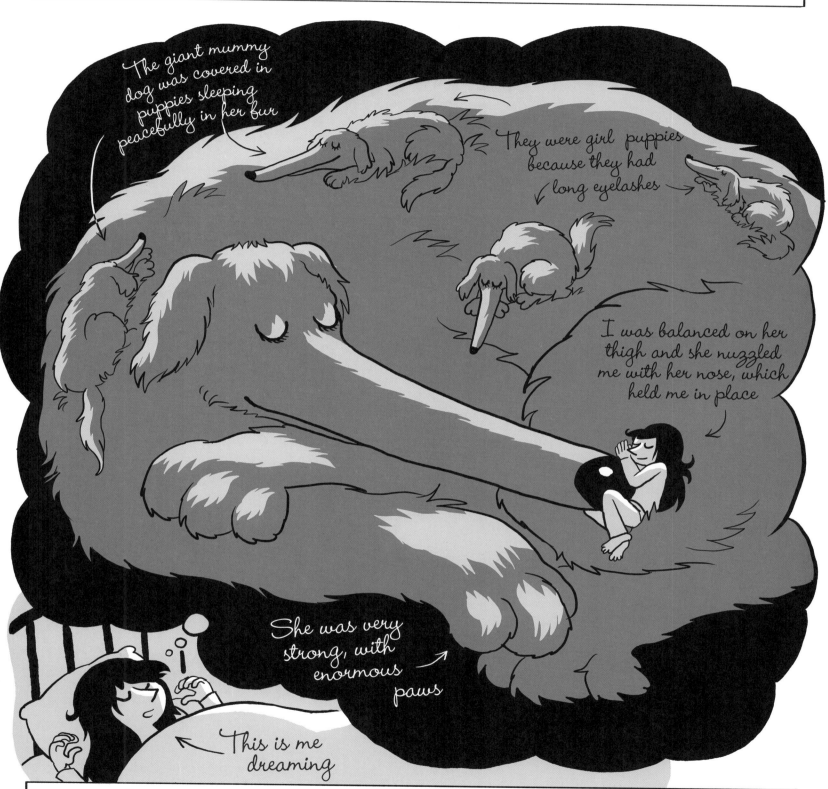

It was a really sweet, cosy dream! And when I woke, I didn't hate dogs any more because I was in, "Wow, I wish I had a mummy dog" mode!

(Based on a true story told by Esther A, who is 11 years old)

Riad Sattouf

Rapping

I can't wait to be 18. Seriously. I'm counting the days. Time passes waaay too slowly.

When I'm 18, the first thing I'll do is leave this family and go away so I never have to see my brother again.

My parents will complain but I'll leave anyway.

I'll live in a tiny apartment with my friend Cassandra and we'll eat junk food all day and be happy.

I'll go out every night with my friends if I feel like it...

... or with my boyfriend.

The years will go by. The only one I'll see regularly is my dad. I'll have my dream job by then: editor of bestselling YA novels.

He'll weep with admiration at my incredible success.

Then will come the sad day when, after many years, my mum dies. And at her funeral, I'll see my older brother again.

Weakened by his endless failures, he'll try to patch things up with me.

When he dies, I'll pay for his gravestone. Well, not the whole thing (they're expensive) but the plaque that goes on top of it.

(Based on a true story told by Esther A, who is 11 years old)

Riad Sattouf

Bastille Day

My parents have gone to London for the weekend in "we're so in love" mode, my big brother has gone to stay with his friend Lucien (an idiot, just like him), and my grandmother has taken my little brother with her to Brittany. I stayed here for the weekend at my friend Cassandra's apartment. She lives in Saint-Denis (a town far away) but we went to see the Bastille Day fireworks in Paris at the Pont des Arts (it wasn't great — we couldn't see anything). We heard some teenagers say, "There's been an attack, it's really bad," so we wanted to look at Cassandra's phone but her mum confiscated it. Apparently what happened was really horrible but I don't know what it was because we didn't have time to see. Cassandra was really scared so when we got back to her room she said, "We have to build my dad's house." And I was like, "Huh?"

(Based on a true story told by Esther A, who is 11 years old)

Riad Sattouf

The Secret of Cars

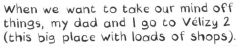

Panel 1: When we want to take our mind off things, my dad and I go to Vélizy 2 (this big place with loads of shops).

This is me and him in "let's buy stuff" mode

Panel 2: Hey, sweetie, you see that car in front? That's a Tesla... You don't see many of those, they're electric...

It's an American car

Panel 3: What do you mean, it's American?

Hang on, are you saying that not all cars are made in the same place?

I mean it's made in America! Our car's a Renault, it's French...

Panel 4: I must admit I'd never thought that cars could come from other countries! To be honest it's a subject I have, like, subzero interest in (LOL).

Seriously Esther? What did you think? That all cars just come from "the car factory"? They're like clothes, there are different brands...

FOR REAL, YO?

Baby, you know you're not supposed to say "yo" any more

Panel 5: It was bizarre. In fact I'd NEVER looked at cars before! So, did you know that there are Japanese cars called TSUSHI or something? We saw some!

They're tiny but quick

Even smaller in real life

Panel 6: And then there are German cars (Mercedes)...

They're, like, huge

Very old driver

Massive wheels

Panel 7: ... Italian cars (Fiat Runto or something)...

Cube-shaped

Realistic drawing

Panel 8: ... and English cars (Jaguar, like the animal!). Each country has its own brand.

But jaguars don't live in England...

That's not logical

WELL SPOTTED

Panel 9: My dad always says that our family isn't French but BRETON (the name for people from Brittany).

So are there Breton cars?

REALLY?

Of course! The famous Seagull 22

Panel 10: He told me that it was an amphibious car (that means it goes on water).

Brilliant idea!

Panel 11: ... and you could sail it like a boat!

I want one when I'm older

Pure freedom!

Panel 12: In fact it was all just my dad's fantasy (that means a lie). But it really made me laugh!

I totally kiffe it when he says crazy stuff

HA HA

AND WHEN YOU HONK THE HORN IT SCREECHES LIKE A SEAGULL

♡ ♡ ♡ ♡ I LOVE HIM ♡ ♡ ♡ ♡

(Based on a true story told by Esther A, who is 11 years old)

Riad Sattouf

Prawns

Have you ever heard of these things called "prawns"?

This is me as a baby eating them

Yum yummm

My dad feeding me (look at his hairstyle)

Prawns are creatures that live underwater and that some people like to eat.

MORE PAWN

I loved them when I was little

But now I think they're the most disgusting things in the world.

The other day in the street I thought about how they tasted and I almost threw up

Bleurgh

Salty, soft, rubbery, gross

In fact, to me...

... a prawn and a cockroach **are the same thing, yo**

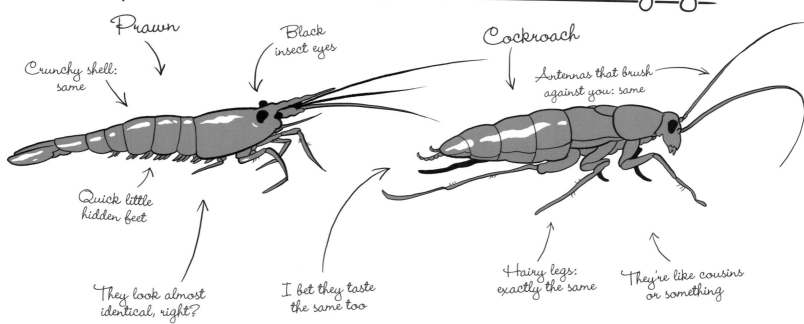

Prawn

Black insect eyes

Cockroach

Crunchy shell: same

Antennas that brush against you: same

Quick little hidden feet

They look almost identical, right?

I bet they taste the same too

Hairy legs: exactly the same

They're like cousins or something

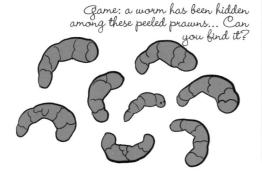

Not only that but when you peel them they look like little caterpillars or worms...

Game: a worm has been hidden among these peeled prawns... Can you find it?

My dad adores them. When he eats them, he SUCKS THEIR HEADS.

MLMM

SLURP!

KKRNCH

MLMM

SLURP!

KKRNCH

(Based on a true story told by Esther A, who is 11 years old)

Riad Sattouf

The Wedding

Of course I DREAM of getting married one day, when I've become a grown-up.

This is me watching some newlyweds in the park near our house

A wedding is something that joins two lovers for eternity.

It's a sacred oath for all humans, wherever they're from

You have to love each other and you must never cheat, because you both wear a WEDDING RING on one finger to remind you of your vows.

Gold rings that the bride and groom put on each other's fingers

The only thing I don't like about weddings is that the girl has to wear a white dress.

I'd wear trousers and a blouse with "explosive" coloured patterns because I think it's funny

I'd carry my bouquet like this (rebel bride, yo LOL)

Definitely high heels though

My future husband will be good-looking and thrilled by the idea of loving nobody but me until he dies.

Blond, why not? I love blond hair

He has to wear the traditional black suit and tie though (I'm the boss! Just kidding...)

I'd invite loads of people to my wedding. Family, friends, schoolmates...

They'll all be there to congratulate me

Even Eugenie

My parents and brothers

I've already been married twice before. But thankfully I got unmarried straight away each time.

I'm not going to join with someone for eternity when I'm just a kid

It was a "game"

WHOOOO

Divorce is a terrible tragedy that brings a marriage to an end. It's the death of love. I have some friends whose parents are divorced but who aren't upset about it. Worse, some of them are actually happy (Violette, for example).

Divorce is great! I have two homes now and I get twice as many Christmas and birthday presents!

My parents were married before I was born.

My mum wearing white, of course

My dad looking sooo handsome

I don't think I'd survive if my parents got divorced. I'm so scared of it. I think about it all the time when they argue, even just a little bit.

Don't add too much sugar to the cake this time...

Yeah well last time there wasn't enough!

But it'll be too sweet and you...

I LIKE IT WHEN IT'S...

You're not going to get divorced are you?

Then they look at me in "our daughter's such a worrier" mode and they smile

(Big relief — I was really worried)

(Based on a true story told by Esther A, who is 11 years old)

Riad Sattouf

The Betrothed

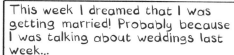

This week I dreamed that I was getting married! Probably because I was talking about weddings last week...

This is me just before the dream (I'd eaten too much ravioli)

public

I was in this really beautiful forest with loads of little super-cute furry animals around. They were leading me to my WEDDING.

HURRAH!

She's getting hitched!

This way, Esther!

Esther! Quick, to the altar!

After a while, I came to a clearing and I saw my husband waiting for me! I was super-happy because he was really good-looking (with wild, longish hair, like an art student or something)...

There he is! There he is, your BETROTHED!

I loved him _immediately_

I went over to him and then... OMG!

Um...

There you are, my love

Let's go to the altar

Yep, he was TINY!

I was panicking but I kept it hidden because this was my wedding and I didn't want to hurt his feelings. But I was thinking, "How can I spend eternity with such a small man?"

THEY'RE GETTING MARRIED!

YAAAY!

THEY'RE GETTING MARRIED!

The furry creatures were so happy

Afterwards we went to the house and the bed was cardboard and the pillows were paper and it was so enormous that we got lost in it.

So anyway, the next morning was weird... I was still looking for my husband... and I found my mum and my little brother sitting on the sofa reading a musical book for babies.

Press the button for the song!

Gooh

♪ He was a little man!
He was a little man!
And he had a funny house! ♪

The house was made of cardboard! The house was made of cardboard! The stairs were made of paper! The stairs were made of paper!

Come on Esther, sing with us! "He was a little man..."

(Based on a true story told by Esther A, who is 11 years old)

Riad Sattouf

Summer Camp

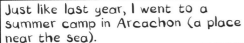

Just like last year, I went to a summer camp in Arcachon (a place near the sea).

This is me, Cassandra and my parents on the train station platform

I was so happy to be bringing Cassandra with me! We'd never gone anywhere together before.

We've always been in the same primary school but soon we'll be going to different secondary schools (so sad!)

We were going to make the most of this holiday!

We stood in front of the woman with the list of kids going to the camp, and then disaster struck!

Nope, sorry, there's no Cassandra on my list!

So basically it was my mum who made the reservations on the internet and she messed up (typical her). I was the only one who could go.

Esther, yes. Cassandra, nope.

Are you kidding me?

Not at all!

She thought it was funny!

Then Cassandra's mum just burst into tears and started yelling!

WHAAT?

Take her! Please!

I can't. We're full.

But what am I supposed to do? I have a job, I can't look after her!

I understand, madame, but she's not on the list. There's nothing I can do.

TAKE HER!

The woman said the only way she could go was if someone else pulled out. So we waited. I got angry and shouted at my mum.

IF SHE DOESN'T GO, I'M NOT GOING, YO!

We watched people turn up one after another. It was like a nightmare.

Zinedine...

Yep, you're on the list!

Everybody had made their reservations correctly EXCEPT MY MUM.

I won't leave without you!

Hng! Hng!

After a while, Cassandra started trying to cheer me up!

Don't worry about me Esther! You should go...

Have fun...

At last it was time to leave. I thought I was going to die.

It's okay — one family didn't turn up. You can go.

We hugged all the way to camp

(Based on a true story told by Esther A, who is 11 years old)

Riad Sattouf

110

The Tart

I have a very sweet tooth!

This is me eating sugar straight from the bag

GULP

KRCH KRCH

In "addict" mode

That means like a "junkie"

It was raining the other day and my dad came back from Auchan with a surprise!

Look what I got you, sweetie!

?

MY FAVOURITE FOOD IN THE WHOLE WORLD!

Pfft they're not even in season! Why'd you buy that? It's bad for the planet, you know...

My mum the eternal killjoy

The strawberry tart of my dreams

The strawberries are big and firm and squeezed close together...

They look like jewels or something

Mmmm

I could live on strawberry tarts

... and covered in sweet, sticky, delicious juice

With a biscuity crust and lovely cream on top

And criss-cross designs on the side!

DAD: I LOVE YOU

When I'm grown up, I'll always have a strawberry tart in my fridge.

It'll be my consolation after a tough day at work

Nothing and nobody will stop me eating as much as I want.

I won't have to share it with anyone

KRNCH

KRNNCH

KRRNCH

KRNCH

I'll be an ADULT

And then I'll go to bed happy, thinking about my dad who used to give me tarts like that even out of season because he knew I loved them and his daughter's happiness was more important to him than the "fate of the planet" or whatever...

A tiny nostalgic tear will roll down my cheek (LOL)

(Based on a true story told by Esther A, who is 11 years old)

Riad Sattouf

Secondary School

Can you believe it? I've started secondary school at that free, posh place in the centre of Paris!

This is me in my bed, early in the morning on the first day of school, worrying about what it'll be like

I was afraid of being alone in the corridors of that enormous school, with nobody to help me find my classroom.

I was afraid of not being intelligent enough to understand the classes.

Esther? What's the answer? Didn't you learn anything in primary school?

$$z.12,45\sqrt{xb}$$
$$\frac{(y)\times 45m. \cos}{\sqrt{3,22}\times (b+c)} \frac{}{v+ab}(73.5)$$
$$=?$$

I was afraid the other children would be snooty aristocrats who'd look down on me.

Do you smell something?

Who's that commoner?

They let anybody in nowadays!

I was afraid of being the ugliest girl in a school full of models.

Just kill yourself or something

So I paid great care to what I wore.

Flowery outfit from England given to me by my aunt

So it still feels like summer

Light leather sandals

My dad took me by car (after that, I'll have to take a bus on my own). He was very happy.

There are ministers and presidents who went to this school, you know!

We arrived outside the building and my dad turned to me.

Okay, Esther, you're going to secondary school, so you're now allowed to have a phone.

HERE YOU ARE

FNAC

YAAAAAAAAY

FNAC

A NOKIA?

It's a very good TELEPHONE!

I'd received a letter telling me that I'd be in Class 6A. When I got to the school, I saw someone holding a sign. I didn't get lost. All the other students I saw were really ugly...

I felt less alone (LOL)

6A Wait under this sign

... on the other hand, they all had an iPhone or a Samsung.

And when I say "all," I mean all

6A Wait under this sign

(Yep, even her)

(Based on a true story told by Esther A, who is 11 years old)

Riad Sattouf

112

Part 3
Tales from My 12-Year-Old Life

The First Day

My name is Esther and I'm 11 years old. After going to a private primary school, I'm now in Year 7 at a free-but-posh secondary school in the centre of Paris.

This is me outside my new school in "okay, you're in the big time now" mode

← Belly button showing

In fact, I was supposed to go to a school near where we live, the one my brother goes to.

But it's a ZPEP, a violent place where girls are hassled by stupid boys like him

Yo, I just let one rip for you

Can you smell it?

Esther, you smell that?

But then I took the entrance exam for a very good school in a chic neighbourhood... and I got in! My dad told me I'm very lucky.

I'm a good student and I'm pretty so I think that the school is lucky to have me

Just kidding, yo!

I say that because the kids in my class are really ugly (not that I care, it's just interesting to observe).

This one, for example, has dark fuzzy hair on her top lip and between her eyebrows, but she seems happy

She's wearing "I'm so fashionable" Stan Smith sneakers

This boy looks like a girl. Long hair, high-pitched voice... And he smells like damp laundry...

I sat behind him in one class and had his stink in my nostrils all day long

This one looks like a CHICK (a baby chicken, I mean, not a girl).

Cute and sweet but, you know, I could never be "friends" with that

Then there are some boys from Porch-gull or something. Their mums are caretakers for apartment buildings.

They have almost-footballer hair

Always together

There's only one boy I think is handsome. His name is Louis. Check out his magnificent jawline and how well it goes with his neck!

Black curly hair

Looks open to life

Perfectly straight nose

And he talks to adults like he's the same age or something, like they're equals.

Have you conferred with the other teachers to limit the number of books we have to carry around? So our bags are less heavy?

Good idea!

Ah, that's a shame.

Um, no, I haven't.

Yep, the teachers are ANCIENT!

I was hanging around in the courtyard the other day in "I have a feeling I'm not going to have any friends this year" mode, and he came over to TALK to me!

Hi there, I'm Louis... I hope I'm not disturbing you?

I, uh, no...

He really talks like an adult, right?

I had a question for you... it's probably stupid of me, but... are you the one who plays SOLINE LEPIC in "Fais pas ci, fais pas ça"?

N... No! I...

Wow, you look just like her!

"Fais pas ci, fais pas ça" is a funny TV show about families, and Soline Lepic is one of the characters and she's <u>beautiful.</u>

This is her →

Gorgeous brunette →

Deep, confident voice →

← Playful, flirtatious look

Am I really like her?

THIS BOY IS PERFECT (LOL)

(Based on a true story told by Esther A, who is 11 years old)

Riad Sattouf

Gods

This year, in history, we're studying the Greeks.

This is me pretending to be interested

The Greeks were polytheistic. Who knows what that means?

Polytheism means having lots of different gods. It's a really good idea.

Look at them all!

It's much better than what we have now, where there's just one boy-god...

Like a dictator who knows everything...

I'm in charge of the universe

Posing in "I'm the best" mode

When there's only one god, I feel alone and abandoned. Because if he has to do everything on his own, he's bound to be overworked...

Dear God, please cancel tomorrow's English test, I beg you, Lord

How many people are asking him stuff like that, all at the same time?

So I'm left with the impression that he doesn't do anything.

Sorry, I was busy, I forgot

You have one hour

But the Greeks had a whole team of gods, each taking care of different things, and some of them were GIRLS (they're called goddesses).

Persephone (goddess of spring)

Demeter (goddess of harvests)

Tyche (goddess of luck)

Atë (goddess of mistakes)

I think it's a really good idea to have a goddess exclusively for love, for example: Aphrodite.

A super-hot goddess in a bikini who devotes her life to matters of the heart

Then there were some stupid, pointless gods like Apollo, the god of cool dudes...

Look, he's half naked!

Well, I'm sure there are SOME people who look like that (yeah, right)

It takes all sorts! (LOL)

My favourite goddess is Athena. I love her. She's the goddess of war but also (less famously) wisdom.

I think about her a lot

She's a good role model for us women, I think

The story of her birth is hilarious. One day, Zeus – the king of gods – had a terrible headache, so he asked Hephaestus (the god of metal and weapons) to smash him over the head with an axe (to take the pain away LOL).

Hit me right here...

Okay, boss

And the big lump DID IT.

Better now, boss?

Just then, Athena burst out of Zeus's head wearing armour, in "worship me" mode!

YAAAAAH!

(Based on a true story told by Esther A, who is 11 years old)

Riad Sattouf

116

The New Goddesses

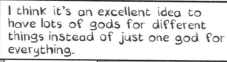

I don't believe in God, but ever since we started studying the Greeks, I've become interested in gods.

This is me as Athena (I adore her)

I think it's an excellent idea to have lots of gods for different things instead of just one god for everything.

I am Everything!

I control Everything!

I know Everything!

Not really likely, is it?

I think we should replace our single-boy-god with some more modern goddesses.

Here are some that I invented!

They were born from my head (LOL)

Wify
Goddess of electronic devices and the internet

Knows all secret codes

Fixes smartphones

Good signal strength

Boyzia
Goddess of relationships with boys

Strong and fights like a boy

Protects weaker girls

Dancy
Goddess of bendiness and sport

You lose weight when you pray to her

Smarta
Goddess of nerds and school

Helps you pass or cancel tests

Aids memory

Athena
Goddess of war and wisdom

Bad-girl-style camouflage

I'm keeping her but modernizing her appearance

Oceania
Goddess of oceans and nature

Breathes underwater

Purifies rivers and seas

Encourages clean, green living

Workina
Goddess of employment

Helps you find a job when you're older

The Great Mother
Goddess of mums

Always surrounded by levitating babies

Nocturna
Goddess of peaceful sleep and sweet dreams

Asleep but she can still hear everything

Uglia
Goddess of people with challenging appearances

Dries their tears and helps them succeed

Goddess of humour

Esther
Goddess of popular people

Just kidding, of course!

(Based on a true story told by Esther A, who is 11 years old)

Riad Sattouf

Trump

In the mornings, my dad wakes my brother and me so we won't be late for school (my mum has already left for work). He's usually in a good mood.

But not this morning →

SOMETHING TERRIBLE'S HAPPENED!

This is me ↓

← Only one eye open

TRUMP HAS BEEN ELECTED PRESIDENT!

YO, nice one, Donald

← My brother the idiot

WHAT? SERIOUSLY?

I must admit I didn't know much about him (I'm not into politics, sorry) but my dad talked about Trump all the time because he was so afraid he'd become president.

and it was around 11 o'clock that Trump moved so far ahead of Clinton that his victory became indisputable

OH GOD ooooooh fucking hell!

Why do you care so much yo?

And then at school everybody was in "Trump is the devil" mode, it was really funny.

IS THERE ANYONE HERE WHO LIKES TRUMP? TELL ME NOW SO I CAN NEVER SPEAK TO YOU AGAIN!

← This Year 8 girl actually shouted that in the courtyard!

And then everybody in class was talking about it and the teacher told off one boy who made a joke about Trump being a duck (his first name is Donald, like the Disney character).

IT WAS A JOKE, SIR, I DON'T LIKE TRUMP

Hmph

Perhaps, but mediocre puns add nothing to the debate.

The president of America is the most powerful leader in the world (I don't know why, apparently that's just how it is), and the Americans just had an election to decide who would take over from Obama, a nice Renoi (that's what us kids call Black people).

The people had to choose between Clinton...

... and Trump →

← I don't know who she is

Everybody thought Clinton was going to win. Everybody. And then, at the last second, Trump was elected.

Those Americans →

I don't know why they didn't think a woman could be president. Anyway...

Trump wants to DESTROY his enemies. He SAYS he's racist (nobody else dares say it), he HATES the Renois, the Rebeus (what us kids call Arab people) and the Noiches (Chinese people). But apparently France is on his list of friends (lucky us).

He looks crazy →

I wouldn't like to be his enemy

You know the weirdest thing though? Donald Trump used to be POLYGAMOUS!

That means he had sex with lots of women he didn't love!

← Un-be-liev-able

← Although it's normal too, I guess: he's a boy

I think everybody's overreacting though. I saw Trump's wife and she seems like a good person. I mean, she used to be a model, and she's 25 while he's 80, so it's obvious that she's manipulating him.

She's, like, a million times too pretty for him

I like her hairstyle →

← Everything in harmony

Straight, thin nose →

Nicely shaped mouth

← Calm and composed

I have a feeling she'll be the one actually running things. What do you think?

Don't worry, Dad. It'll be okay, I'm sure of it.

I hope so, sweetie...

I could tell straight away that my words had soothed him.

(Based on a true story told by Esther A, who is 11 years old)

The Tutorial

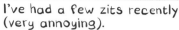

I've had a few zits recently (very annoying).

This is me rummaging through my mum's make-up bag

"Make-up" means hiding imperfections or enhancing facial features with special products made for that purpose.

"Concealer"... Hmm, interesting...

My mum hardly ever wears make-up but she has loads of products that I like to try. Let me show you...

Concealer is a sort of undercoat that hides zits and dark rings

You apply generously then spread it around with the stick

Then you get some foundation and you smear it all over your face.

It's a thick, pink-beige paste that you spread from the centre to the outside

It always makes my face look more tanned than my neck (although with a turtleneck sweater I doubt anyone can tell).

Next, you put on some powder to take the shine off and now I look like I've just come back from my holidays (LOL).

COUGH!

Then you can use some mascara (this black stuff that thickens your eyelashes and makes you look all sultry).

It's really difficult: my hand always trembles when I do it

What if I stick the brush in my eye and blind myself?

Next comes my favourite part: lip gloss (to give you a shiny, swollen-looking mouth).

Sensuality

When I see myself like that, I think I look about 25–30 years old.

Grown woman

FUCK ME THAT'S GROSS YO

Don't move

VLAK

OWW

I like hurting my brother

(Based on a true story told by Esther A, who is 11 years old)

Riad Sattouf

Violence

I'm in Year 7 at a posh school in the centre of Paris. I'm going to change its real name and call it the "ROYAL School" to protect my privacy (and also because I think it's funny).

This is me in "surprise test" mode

To get in, I had to pass a very difficult test because the school I was supposed to go to, near where I live, was full of violence towards girls, and that worried my dad.

Well, God knows what the other school is like because there's loads of violence towards girls at the Royal School
You have five minutes left

Let me tell you what happened to me. There are three Year 9 boys who are all really big and they hang out together in the yard and they're always picking on Year 7 kids.

They talk like rappers and dress like my brother
Sneering
Hoodie
Tracksuit bottoms
Shark sneakers

At the cafeteria, they shake down desserts from other boys. They make it sound like a joke because if not they'd get in trouble.

GIMME THAT YOGHURT, YOU LITTLE QUEER
HAHA
I'M JUST KIDDING...
NOT!
HA HA

Afterwards, in the courtyard, they pretend to be friends with boys from my class...

HEY THERE, MATE!
MAAATE
Hello
HOW ARE YOU DOING, MATE?

... and then they grab them from behind and it almost always ends up in a fight.

A very one-sided fight
HA HA

The other day, I'd had enough of this.

HEY, STOP THAT NOW!
Nobody ever intervenes
?

As soon as I said that, this crowd gathered round us.

Whadja say? Apologize to your master.
Those were his words
NO!

CLAK

WOOOOOOOOH!
WOOOO!

It wasn't a really hard slap but it still knocked my head sideways. I looked around at the people laughing and one of them was THE BOY THAT I'D DEFENDED!

They were beating him up, like, thirty seconds before this! How stupid is he?
Hee hee

So I realized that it's not a place that breeds violence... IT'S BOYS.

If there are any boys reading this page, I have a question for you: WHY DO YOU LIKE VIOLENCE?
ANSWER ME.

(Based on a true story told by Esther A, who is 11 years old)
Riad Sattouf

Smartphones

I thought life in secondary school would be more difficult (in terms of the classes, making friends and new ways of behaving).

This is me and Eva (my new best friend, who I really look up to) monitoring the monitors

Okay, he's gone

All RIGHT! Let's look at Facebook...

My life was turned upside down this week. Let me explain...

Use of mobile phones is banned at my school since three hoodie boys showed some "shocking" pictures to Year 7 kids.

Typical violent, brainless Year 9 boys

Trying to look like warriors or something

But when the father of a Year 7 kid complained, the three boys denied it and there was no proof so they weren't punished... so the whole school has been punished instead. Mobile phones have been banned! (Thanks a lot, you three morons.)

You get a two-day suspension if you're caught with a phone, but we're risking it anyway

All clear

Everybody at my school has a smartphone (with a touch screen and all that).

Except me – I have a Nokia, which is, like, just a phone...

... although it does have a few games

The only smartphones anyone respects here are iPhones. And the one everybody dreams of having is the iPhone 5S (more than the 6 or 7, weirdly).

Yeah, Dad, where are you?

The ones who have them are popular

Yep, even this ugly girl with the monobrow!

She FaceTimes her dad when school is over so everybody will say "Whoa, a 5S..."

I was so ashamed of my Nokia that I would hide it like this when I called my dad after school.

My long hair concealed my shame

Yeah, where are you, Dad?

And then last week, Eva changed my life. That girl is a genius, I swear.

You poor thing... Let me borrow your phone.

She grabbed my Nokia and did this.

SPLUGH

Now see what happens

Result: it still worked, but nobody could hear me when I spoke!

Why doesn't it work any more?

I acted like nothing had happened

My dad was annoyed, but then he went to his room... and came back with his old iPhone 3... and GAVE IT TO ME!

Here, there's no internet but it works!

AND NOW I HAVE AN IPHONE!

And I can even go on the internet because Eva lets me share her network

I can't believe it!

Eva, my saviour!

Yessss!

(Based on a true story told by Esther A, who is 11 years old)

Riad Sattouf

121

The Magic of Christmas

I'm a "list" girl. I write lists all the time. They make life clear and simple. For example, here's my list of everything I love about Christmas.

This is me in the street, thinking about my list

1. The Christmas tree, of course, and the decorations. I love string lights and the reflections on the baubles and the smell of the fir tree.

Our tree always leans to the side but I still love it

2. My 1-year-old brother Gaëtan's face when he looks at the tree.

My little brother in "the most beautiful thing I've ever seen" mode

3. Writing to Father Christmas instead of doing homework.

"Dear Father Christmas, I'd like an iPhone 7 because my iPhone 3 is rubbish. No, just kidding, I know it's too expensive. Um, anything would be great."

4. TV ads for toys — you never see them at any other time of year.

Hey, a toy that makes REAL cakes! WOW!

Smoby Smoby Chef! Mummy we love cakes! Yeaaahh! There are loads of recipes, cool gadgets, and cupcakes...

5. Decorations in the street.

Beautiful "fairy-tale" atmosphere

6. Watching "Santa Claus Is a Stinker" with my dad, who complains he's seen it too many times but always laughs at it.

HAHAHA

IT'S SO FUNNY!

It's Klug, rolled under the armpits

7. All the different chocolates you can only get at Christmas.

Papillotes (delicious)

Kinder Father Christmases (yum)

Lindt Pyrénéens (melt in the mouth!)

Idea: why not sell them all year round?

8. Trying to guess from the shapes of the presents hidden in my parents' cupboard whether they've got us what we wanted.

GAASP! But... is it... an iPhone?

I DAREN'T BELIEVE IT !

9. Criticizing what my parents eat on Christmas Eve.

It's funny seeing his reaction

But Dad, don't you realize you're eating the sick liver of a DEAD BIRD?

A DEAD BIRD!

10. The Yule log, because the idea of it disgusts me every year (wood as a cake: that's just weird, right?) and yet it tastes amazing.

Yum

11. Opening my presents (I didn't want to put this at number 1 because it seems greedy) and being a bit... well, DISAPPOINTED.

Ooh, the new iPhone! That's great!

Esther, are you happy too? Can I taste your cupcakes?

(Based on a true story told by Esther A, who is 11 years old)

Riad Sattouf

Hamster Years

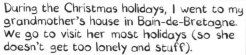

During the Christmas holidays, I went to my grandmother's house in Bain-de-Bretagne. We go to visit her most holidays (so she doesn't get too lonely and stuff).

This is me before I show you something

It's oooookaaaaaay... shh, sweetheart shh, it's oookaaaay...

So... very carefully, I'd like to introduce you...

Shhhh, it's okay

Please welcome ...

... MANUELA.

She's a small "sapphire"-coloured Russian hamster that I got for Christmas.

Look at the size of my thumb next to her

Curious little thing

She's called Manuela in tribute to Manuela Diaz, a little girl from "The Voice Kids" who sings like an angel

I wasn't expecting her at all. I hadn't asked for a pet! She was a gift from my grandmother.

A real animal is so much better than your electronic gadgets, you'll see. But it's a big responsibility!

You can tell she's my father's mother — she thinks like him (LOL)

A Russian hamster is a hamster that comes from Russia apparently. It's a quiet little rodent, smaller than a golden hamster but more elegant and less clumsy (IMO).

A golden hamster

Manuela

My sweet

Honestly, which one do you prefer?

Hamsters live about 2 years apparently. Manuela is 2 months old, which is about 20 in human years.

Manuela, you were born last October and you're already a young woman...

I calculated how old I would be in hamster years, and the answer was 408.

I'm a 408-year-old hamster!

Like, whoooa

Manuela's house
(which I also got as a present)

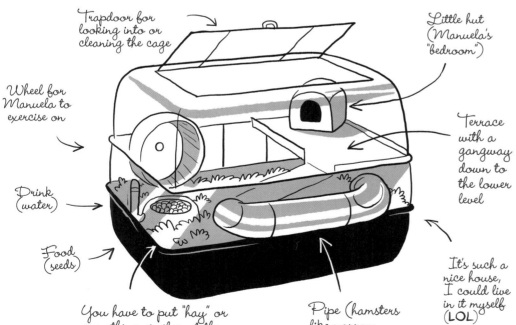

Trapdoor for looking into or cleaning the cage

Little hut (Manuela's "bedroom")

Wheel for Manuela to exercise on

Terrace with a gangway down to the lower level

Drink (water)

Food (seeds)

You have to put "hay" or something similar at the bottom of the cage because hamsters are burrowers (they like to dig)

Pipe (hamsters like narrow tunnels and stuff, don't ask me why)

It's such a nice house, I could live in it myself (LOL)

(Based on a true story told by Esther A, who is 11 years old)

Riad Sattouf

123

The Gay Teacher

I'm not a problem student. I mean, I always do my homework even if I don't feel like it, in "I have to do it anyway so why kick up a fuss?" mode.

This is me sensing that I'm going to get a good mark in French

All riiiight... I've marked your stories! So many good things, genuinely! I am thrilled. Apparently, my dears, you were truly inspired by the story of Ariadne and the Minotaur...

So... the best story of all was by...

Can you guess?

YES, ESTHER, OF COURSE HAHA!

The kids in my class think the French teacher is gay (they call him a "queer" but I think that's insulting).

Everybody hates him because of that. And it's true, he is really annoying with his little expressions and his "touchy-feely" personality.

17/20 for my little Esther

He, like, totally adores me. It's so embarrassing.

Compelling, amusing, your story is wonderful. And I loved the "Minotaur" that you brought in at the end.

Oh what a pretty blue folder...

?!?

Blue is my favourite colour.

People think a boy shouldn't say he loves a colour in front of everybody like that... It's girls who are supposed to express their feelings...

Blue is my favourite colour

Ha ha

Lea, 15, very good.

Boys are supposed to be tough and mysterious.

Like Louis

You never know what he's thinking

Deep, dark aura

If boys start acting like girls, what will girls have left?

All riiiight my dears, let's get to work now!

Seriously, can't he just shut up?

A boy is a boy and a girl is a girl. Nobody likes it when the two get mixed up. Well, I don't anyway.

ESTHER!

Louis?!?

Esther, don't you think it's weird the way the teacher talks to you? Watch yourself because he looks like he wants to RAPE you!

Sorry if you find that shocking but that's what he said

Why did he have to say that? Now I'm scared

And blue is my favourite colour too!

(Based on a true story told by Esther A, who is 11 years old)

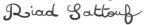

124

The Fresh Tune

There's a totally fresh (that means good) tune at the moment that everybody loves. It's the new single by Black M.

This is me watching the video and thinking I should show it to Dad so he'll change his mind about Black M

Black M is a very good-looking rapper. I didn't used to listen to his stuff because my stupid brother liked it, but actually his new song is really good.

Just watch and listen, Dad!

Black M? Is that what you use your phone for?

I adore my dad but he hates young people's music

It's called "French Kiss" and it's about... well, I'm not sure but it's definitely not about kissing.

It starts with a Renoi child in a kitchen who hears someone knock at the door

And when he opens it he sees this incredibly beautiful girl (my age, I think).

She has dreadlocks, a Renoi hairstyle, but she's Babtou (that means white)

Gorgeous

Too proud to admit your feelings, It's wrong to playyyy...

After that, they drink some Innocent orange juice (that's a brand).

Whoa, product placement ha ha!

Daaad!

Then they're under a duvet and the girl is making these really beautiful "weird" movements.

She is SO pretty

stop messing around

In the morning, the girl brings him breakfast and there's another bottle of Innocent orange juice!

Is this an ad for orange juice or what?

DAD! Just be quiet and listen!

Sorry

I still don't think I'm a fan though

And then she's in the bath, dreaming about a rubber duck.

One lost, ten foooouuuuund

The look on her face isn't very "childlike"

And after that they laugh like crazy in "we're disguised as robots" mode.

I love her a little a lot French kiss

And after THAT they do this really impressive "hip-hop" dance (the best kind of dancing in the world but also the hardest) and you understand that they're actually these amazing dancers.

I love her passionately French kiss

Dad, would it bother you if I had dreadlocks?

When you're 18? Not at all!

My dad is sooo funny

We walked through the fruit juice aisle and I saw a bottle of Innocent. I didn't ask my dad if we could buy some because I knew what he would say LOL.

But it did look really good

(Based on a true story told by Esther A, who is 11 years old)

Riad Sattouf

125

The Illness

I really like winter. This time of year makes me laugh because my dad gets SO stressed out.

This is me coming home from school in "I'm going to tease him" mode

DAD! GIVE ME A HUG!

ESTHER! WHAT DO WE DO WHEN WE COME IN FROM OUTDOORS?

"We don't wash our hands and we lick our fingers after they've touched the metal poles in the metro"

SCHLRPSSS

ESTHER THAT'S DISGUSTING, YOU...

Just kiddiiing! Look, clean hands!

I used this

Hand sanitizer

BAG

My dad is strong and muscular (he doesn't fear anyone) and intelligent (he passed his bac) and sensitive (cries while watching TV sometimes) but he is WAY too scared of germs.

Dad, you're crazy

AHHH, good girl! Hey, let me have some!

Slurp

He's worried that I'll get a stomach bug, which can make you vomit and/or have diarrhoea... Stomach bugs usually last 2 or 3 days and they're very contagious.

You can catch it by shaking hands

Or from someone breathing

Every time someone with a stomach bug flushes the toilet, a thousand million germs are released

Door handle covered in germs (invisible)

My dad says the French are disgusting because they never wash their hands after going to the toilet.

I must admit none of the girls in my school wash their hands

PSCHHH

VZRB

He says France is the only country where there are epidemics of stomach bugs. In other countries, everybody washes their hands apparently.

On the train to Brittany, I saw this old woman flush the toilet and leave, but I DIDN'T hear the tap run.

CLAK

SSSHHH

YU-UCK

And she was in first class too (for rich people)

What's funny (although also sad) is that despite all his precautions, my dad is always catching stomach bugs at his gym.

Are you okay, Dad?

Yes, yes... Esther, I'm on the toilet, just leave me in peace

---

Afterwards, he has to eat potatoes and drink flat Coke and my brother Antoine cruelly mocks him.

You don't wash your hands properly, yo, it's disgusting, ha ha

My poor suffering father

Anyway, we all end up getting it from him.

And it's obvious that he blames himself

So...

People of France, please wash your hands

(Based on a true story told by Esther A, who is 11 years old)

Riad Sattouf

The Crime Syndicate

My school is a free school where all the students are from very rich families (correction: all but me).

This is me in the courtyard in "yup, I think it's winter" mode

So anyway, the other day Big Baby (that's my nickname for a boy in my class who looks like a big baby) came to see me and said:

Um, Esther, could you lend me 2 euros?

You can have it back next week I promise

Not so long ago he laughed at me after I'd defended him from these bullies, so I just said, "No, go away."

He went straight to someone else

Excuse me! Can you lend me 2 euros? You'll get it back, I promise

Then Eva (my best friend) came to see me. She was laughing.

Hey, what's going on? All the Year 7 boys are trying to borrow money!

IT WAS, LIKE, REALLY WEIRD.

All the Year 7 boys were asking girls for money

After a while, one of the nerds complained to a monitor.

Sir, he's trying to get money off me!

Then things got out of hand!

At this school there are three punks in Year 9 who are always getting into trouble

Now don't ask me why, but two Year 10 boys started copying their style and now they are punks too.

Before, they were like this:

And now they're like this:

And they've become the bosses of the Year 9 punks. They asked them for money to buy stuff, so the Year 9 punks asked the Year 7 boys to find them some money.

They were called the "Boyz 4 Crime gang"

You have to write "four" as "4" because that's how it is on the street (and I must admit I like it)

After Big Baby got in trouble, the headmaster put an end to the gang's activities. But there was no evidence against the punks, so only the Year 7 kids were punished.

They always get away with it

Very cunning

But apparently Big Baby has received threats. He was the one who tried to snitch on the punks after someone snitched on him and now they want to kill him.

Now, after school, he hurries to his parents' car

BIG BABY IS 4 IT NOW!!!

(I know it's not funny for him but still)

(Based on a true story told by Esther A, who is 11 years old)

Riad Sattouf

The Life Test

It was my birthday this week and now I'm 12! It's funny because at my school we had the medical visit (it only happens in Year 7 apparently) and it was like I was taking a "life test" or something. Two nurses measured me and stuff while asking me scientific/personal questions ("Do you have any family problems? Have you ever taken drugs? Have you had your period?"). This gave me the idea of making a progress report on myself for a joke (I love talking about myself, I must admit LOL).

Me at 12

Hair: thick and luxuriant

Height: 5 ft.! Not tall, not short, just normal. Need to keep growing (minimum height for a model: 5 ft. 9 in.)

Weight: 90 lbs. Yes, I'm telling you my weight — I'm a modern girl

A bit pigeon-toed (not too badly)

Nose: straight (thankfully)

Head: leans forward a bit (but I always lift it up, imagining that there's a thread pulling on it — a technique I learned in dance class)

Arms: slender and graceful (I like my arms)

Legs: too thin (they make an L with my too-big feet)

Feet: size 3 (and Stan Smiths start at 4, so I have to be patient LMAO)

Pretty even from behind (yes, I love myself — well, it's better than hating myself, right?)

My complex: I have some white spots at the edge of my nose

Yeah, you can see I'm pigeon-toed

Nurse's verdict: I am normal

Should I change my hairstyle to celebrate?

Braids? A bit "little girl"

Bob? Too "Goody Two-shoes"

Cornrows? Daring — I like it

Pageboy? I love this

Go back to a ponytail?

Oh, and my eyesight is excellent. I took an eye exam and I could see everything

Can you read this? If not, call the doctor!

Now I'm 12, I'll finally be able to watch the film "50 Shades of Grey", a scandalous movie about an all-consuming passion, forbidden to under-12s!

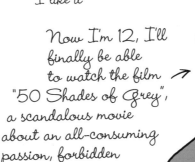

Handsome and tough

Submissive and passionate

(Just kidding — I don't really want to see it LOL)

(Based on a true story told by Esther A, who is 12 years old)

Riad Sattouf

The Review

Did you know that I'm a world-famous celebrity? Okay, that's a slight exaggeration (I'm funny, right?)

This is me feeling pretty pleased about my 19/20 in French, tapping in the code to get into our apartment building

For the past two and a half years I've been telling stories about my life to a cartoonist friend of my dad's and he makes them into books.

A new volume just came out and I read it

To be honest I never read "Esther's Notebooks" in the newspaper where it appears. I always forget, even though my dad gets that paper. I read them in book form instead.

This is what I think of the new one:

It's a very realistic depiction of my life (tastes, hairstyle changes, relationships with friends and lovers)

Although...

Although, if you want to know the truth, I don't really watch my language at school (I just say whatever I want) so I use far more swear words in real life than in the book.

For example in the first panel of page 21 in that book, it's like this:

My brother Antoine goes to a free (but really violent) school. Thankfully, I escaped it.

This is me with Cassandra trying to avoid Eugenie in the playground

Let's pretend we haven't seen her

Yeah

But in real life, it'd be more like:

My brother Antoine goes to a free (but really violent) school. Thankfully, I escaped it.

This is me with Cassandra trying to avoid Eugenie in the playground

C'mon, we don't give a shit about her

Yeah

Or in panel 2 on page 15:

We each had to take one of our old toys so they could be given to a poor child.

I brought my Cicciobello...

Really? You didn't want to keep it?

It's a doll that talks if you put batteries in it

Pfft, it's a baby toy!

And the truth:

We each had to take one of our old toys so they could be given to a poor child.

I brought my Cicciobello...

Really? You didn't want to keep it?

It's a doll that talks if you put batteries in it

Nah, I don't give a shit about it!

Honestly, everybody says "I don't give a shit". It means "I don't care"

You can also say "I don't give a flying fuck"

I say that a lot.

"I DON'T GIVE A FLYING FUCK"

I know what "fuck" means... It's how babies are made.

But I'm not sure about a flying fuck.

How would that work?

To be honest I never read "Esther's Notebooks" in the newspaper where it appears. I always forget, even though my dad gets that paper. I read them in book form instead.

This is what I think of the new one:

It's a very realistic depiction of my life (tastes, hairstyle changes, relationships with friends and lovers)

Although... I don't really give a shit!

(Based on a true story told by Esther A, who is 12 years old)

Riad Sattouf

129

Religions

Sorry if you're shocked by this but no, I still don't believe in God or in religions or any magic stuff at all really.

This is me laughing at these subjects

Ha ha "God"! I mean, come on...

It's not a subject that interests me (my favourite subjects are things like "music", "fashion" and "the art of living") but everybody in my school is in "God exists" mode.

These are the religions that I know about:

1. The Estherians. I'm their goddess...

Just kidding

1. The Christians. Their god is called, well, "God", and their lives seem to revolve around that.

Me if I was Christian

Oh how I adore little baby Jesus!

Eugenie, an ex-friend of mine, used to dress like this

You can get cursed in this religion if you disobey Jesus (the Christians' prophet) because he died "for us" or something, but that's all I know.

You have to pray like this if you're a Christian, with a wooden cross round your neck

Forgive me, Lord

Yeah, this type of cross

2. The Jews. Their god is Yahweh, and all I know is that they have loads of holidays (good idea) and that some Jewish men dress in black and wear big hats and have hair hanging down by their ears.

Me if I was Jewish

Yay, a holiday!

I saw this in an old film, "Rabbi Roger" or something

People often think I'm Jewish because apparently Esther is a Jewish name.

Esther! Oh, so you're a Jewish person

YEAH!

Ah, cool

Actually, NO!

HA HA

I think it's really funny, sorry

3. The Muslims. Their god is Allah and that's all I know. Terrorists are often mostly Muslim but that doesn't mean that all TERRORISTS are Muslim.

Me if I was Muslim

Some Muslim women hide their hair with a headscarf, that's the law. I've seen it on TV I think and I always see girls like this in the supermarket

Sorry, what I meant was "that doesn't mean that all MUSLIMS are terrorists" (it was a stupid mistake because I don't know anything about it, I'm sorry, please forgive me if I offended anyone).

Sorry again. I am just a child ♥

4. The Buddhists. I don't know the name of their god and I don't know anything about what they do except that they wear red cloths and spend ages meditating.

Me if I was a Buddhist

You have to put your fingers like this

Meditating is staying completely still and calm and living in the present moment intensely and in "no stress" mode.

That's totally me! I'm a natural Buddhist!

(LOL)

So that's all the religions I know. And I find it weird that they all fight each other when they all have the same god. Well, yeah, there's only one god!

Although, as a non-believer, it's probably a bit weird for me to say that...

I'm very tired...

So just ignore everything I said and worship whatever god you like. Let's talk about something else...

I'm going to watch "Une saison au zoo" on France 4.

Girl completely uninterested by the subject of religion (LOL)

(Based on a true story told by Esther A, who is 12 years old)

The Candidates

I got really stressed out this week.

This is me listening to my dad in "him talking as usual mode" when suddenly...

If Marine Le Pen is elected, we're moving to Belgium!

On my mother's life that's what he said ("on my mother's life" means "I swear". — It's the language of the street, yo!)

Apparently we're having an election soon to choose a new French president (I didn't realize because I'm not allowed to watch TV).

The president at the moment is François Hollande

Fairly okay I think

So I started taking an interest in politics because I REALLY don't want to live anywhere else.

This is what I know about the presidential candidates

And what I think of their looks

Because that's important.

1. FRANÇOIS FILLON

Good-looking for his age (old)

But he's on the right (doesn't like the poor, prefers the rich)

Might go to prison in fact because he gave his wife loads of money and it wasn't allowed (don't ask me why it wasn't allowed)

Chances of becoming president: zero

2. MANUEL VALLS

Not bad, but too skinny

Also on the right I think

I don't know much about him

Apparently has a good chance of winning

3. ALAIN JUPPÉ

If he had hair, he'd be okay

Hates Fillon (an old feud or something)

Also on the right

Chances of being president: a bit

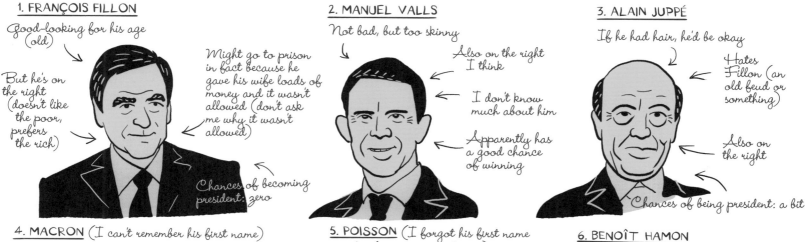

4. MACRON (I can't remember his first name)

Never seen his face so I can't judge

All I know is he's "in the race"

On the right (yep, him too LOL)

Chances of being elected: unlikely if nobody knows who he is

5. POISSON (I forgot his first name too, but his surname is funny)

Apparently he'd be a dictator (although I could be wrong)

On the left

"President Fish" (LMAO)

Chances of becoming president: impossible

6. BENOÎT HAMON

Physically: not my type

BUT

I'd vote for him if I could because he said that if he was elected he'd give money to everybody every month, just to make them happy you know, and I like that idea

7. MARINE LE PEN

I won't say anything about her looks but I put her in last place so you can guess what I think of her

I don't know if she's left or right but she must be bad because my dad's scared of her

She doesn't like anybody except Trump (and who likes Trump? He's CRAZY)

She could also go to prison (like Fillon) but I don't know why. Maybe because she's too cruel? Nah, just kidding

Chances of being elected president: ENORMOUS APPARENTLY!

I don't have anything against Belgium (I don't even know where it is) but I really really really don't want to live there.

So now I say this prayer every evening

Dear God, please don't let Marine Le Pen be elected and on my mother's life I'll believe in You. Amen.

(Based on a true story told by Esther A, who is 12 years old)

Riad Sattouf

President Esther

I love imagining other lives for myself. So this is what I'd do if I was president of France (LOL)!

WITH ESTHER
FRANCE WON'T BE SILENCED!

This is me on the day of my election dressed in "feminine and dynamic" mode

1. I'd choose only girls to work with me. Girls are much more intelligent than boys (IMO).

I'd choose them based on their brains, not their looks

2. I'd crack down on terrorists. They're always attacking people and it's really scary.

Apparently the police know who they all are already

DON'T MOVE, SCUM!

But I didn't attack anybody!

YEAH, BUT MAYBE YOU WERE GOING TO, WHO KNOWS!

I'd arrest them before they did it (logical, right?)

3. I'd create special periods where really expensive things went on sale.

I hereby declare the "iPhone 7 for 2 euros" period open!

BRAVO!

HURRAH!

LONG LIVE THE PRESIDENT!

Help yourselves!

4. I'd stop boys insulting and harassing people. All the world's problems are caused by boys in fact.

HEY, PUNK! YOU JUST CALLED A GIRL A "DIRTY HO" FOR THE MILLIONTH TIME! YOU'RE GOING TO PRISON!

AND IT WAS THE PRESIDENT TOO!

5. I'd give children more holidays.

Hi Esther, it's Angela Merkel, I...

Umm, can you call me back on Monday? I'm on holiday

I'd take loads of time off too (LOL)

6. I'd give raises to people who don't get paid much.

My monthly wage just went up from 2,000 euros to... to... 16,500 euros... Oh thank you, Esther, that's so good of you

No problem, Dad!

I am president after all

7. Everybody – foreigners, Renois, Rebeus, whoever – would be allowed to come and live in France if they wanted. Except boys, who'd be "chosen on merit" (basically only the nice ones would be allowed in).

My dear compatriots. Whether they're Babtou, Renoi, Rebeu, Asian or whatever, boys are still BOYS and it's my duty to protect us from them.

8. If Trump tried to call me, I wouldn't answer the phone (because he's horrible and he only works with men anyway). He hates women (apparently he has a mental perversion or something).

President Trump on the line again...

Tell him I don't give a shit and then hang up.

9. I'd destroy the Élysée and build a much better building instead (less "château", you know?).

More ecological or whatever

With trees and stuff growing on it

10. I'd improve the sewers so we'd have fewer floods.

I don't know why really, it just seems important

BUT MOST IMPORTANT OF ALL: I'd try to be a "funny" president so people would like me (all humans love to laugh, right?).

...and so I told Putin, "Yeah, you might be muscly and have atomic bombs and all that... but you're, like, TOTALLY BALD!"

PRESIDENT

HA HA HA HA HA HA

(Based on a true story told by Esther A, who is 12 years old)

Riad Sattouf

Zumba

When I was young, I was really into dance. I took classes and stuff and I really liked it (and apparently I was very gifted). I wanted to be a dancer when I grew up.

This is me in "I don't have time for dance now, I'm in secondary school" mode

So the other day, I went with my mum to her Zumba class to take my mind off things (you know: school, human cruelty, how boring my life is, etc.).

I was happy to do something with my mum

She's getting fit again (phew!)

We went into this room full of old, overweight women (except for me and the teacher) and it started.

BOOM BOOM BOOM BOOM BOOM BOO

Sorry, I meant "except for me, the teacher and my mum"

BOOM ♪ BOOM ♪ BOOM ♪ BOOM ♪ BOOM ♪ BOOM ♪ BOOM ♪ BOOM ♪ BOOM ♪ BOOM ♪ BOOM ♪ BOOM ♪ BOOM ♪ BOOM ♪ BOOM
ZUMBA EVERYBODY DANCE ZUMBA HOT SOUND POUND IN THE BACKGROUND ZUMBA TO THRILL AND TO CHILL YO ZUMBA GOTTA LOVE THAT HOT SOUND POUNDING YO MAMMA MIA YOU'RE GONNA KIFFE IT ZUMBA YEAH ZUM-BA

x4　　x4　　x2　　x2　　x2

It was totally fresh and it all came back to me, like I'd never stopped

While we were dancing I watched my mum and she was doing really well and I was so happy.

ZOUM-BA HEY ZOUM-BA HA

And suddenly I saw this incredible man

ZOUM-BA HOT SOUND POUNDING

A MOUSE-MAN WITH A MONKEY'S BODY OR SOMETHING

On my mother's life he looked like this

Total mouse head

Effeminate

Hairy like a monkey

He was making these movements and I couldn't tell my mum because we were dancing!

READY TO DANCE YO YOUR BODY HOT AND CLOSE COME TO ME BABE

Afterwards I tried to see him again but there was a crowd of people and he'd disappeared!

MUM! Did you see the guy with the mouse head?

Huh?

DREAM OR REALITY?

WHAT HAPPENED, YO?

(Based on a true story told by Esther A, who is 12 years old)

Riad Sattouf

The Future

I often think about the future and stuff. The future is what hasn't happened yet but might happen later. There are films about the future but I think they're all rubbish (dark/scary – not very positive). I don't understand why everybody always imagines that things are going to get worse and worse when there's no way to be sure. Why not imagine the future in "optimistic" mode? That's what I'm going to do (why not?). So it's the year 2100 and I'm 95 years old...

I'd really like to be an editor when I'm older because everybody says I have loads of imagination and I'm good at world-building and stuff... What do you think? Honestly?

(Based on a true story told by Esther A, who is 12 years old)

Riad Sattouf

Dictators

I didn't used to care about politics, but I've changed and now I follow what's going on in the world.

This is me and my parents watching a TV debate among all the people who want to be president

My dad told me that if Marine Le Pen wins, we'll move to Belgium (yep, he was serious) so – since I really don't want to do that – I'm trying to work out how to fight against her (I admit I had no idea who she was).

Yeah, she's actually a woman

Afterwards I was a bit surprised (I'd never seen her talk before). I thought she seemed quite nice in fact (sorry if you're offended by that).

She was probably pretending

She smiled sometimes

Because my dad told me she wants to be the dictator of France

You could tell that she would like to be a dictator (that means deciding everything and ordering everyone about).

She saw everything in black and white and never agreed with anybody (in "I know best" mode)

I thought dictators didn't exist any more, but in fact they do. Trump, for example, really really wants to be a dictator.

But apparently he's so crap that he can't manage it, because the Americans won't let him

So he plays golf all the time instead

Then there's Putin in Russia (he likes Trump and Marine Le Pen). Unlike Trump, he's definitely managed to become a dictator.

He gives orders and nobody dares disobey because they don't want to die

I saw a picture of him riding a bear. He's scary because he's not scared of anything.

This is a real photo – just google "Putin and bear"

Look at him!

There's a dictator in Turkey too. His name is El Dog or something (sorry, I don't think that's actually his name).

I don't know anything about him

And I don't really want to (LOL)

He says bad things about us. He hates us but I don't know why.

President Esther, President El Dog has insulted France again, what should we do?

Send him a photo of one of our atomic bombs with this message:

"STOP IT NOW, EL DOG."

I couldn't be a dictator. I wouldn't be capable of forcing people to do stuff.

I've decided to take money from the rich and give it to the needy.

I'm the president of the AOVRP* and we refuse to give money to the poor. It's our money and we want to keep it.

*ASSOCIATION OF VERY RICH PEOPLE

Oh! I understand. But what about this: for one day, you can swap lives with a poor person. So you can experience how it feels to be penniless. And then we'll talk. What do you say?

Hm, I'd never thought of that!

Okay! Let's try it.

FORCE THEM? NO! MAN-IP-YOU-LATE THEM! (LMAO)

(Based on a true story told by Esther A, who is 12 years old)

Riad Sattouf

Boys and Girls

You want to know the truth? Okay then, here goes: boys are superior to girls. There, I said it.

This is me doing my hair in the morning so I look presentable at school

For a start, it's boys who decide whether a girl is pretty or ugly.

That's life, you just have to accept it

Boys talk about girls with other boys (judging their looks, style, coolness, etc.) and the "chosen" ones become popular.

Just to reassure you...

... I'm one of the popular girls.

Boys also decide who the most popular boys are. Once they've been chosen, they become a sort of leader and the girls start to love them.

They're tall and mature (that means "adult for their age")

None of them are small

It's not unfair, that's just how it is. Boys are stronger, so they're in charge.

Well, I'm stronger than my brother even though he's a boy...

Move or I'll destroy you

Leave me alone

... but I think that's pretty rare

Girls who fight against boys are called "feminists". That's okay, but I think they're overreacting a bit because, here in France, girls can still do loads of things.

Yep, sometimes I'm ALONE in my neighbourhood dressed like this and nothing bad happens

I think all we need to do to make life better for women in France is to stop boys acting like punks.

MWAAH♪

Yo... ho?

Don't tell me you're surprised by this!

... but I don't give a shit

This is punk behaviour

My dad has a gay female cousin. I love her but she's always lecturing me about feminism. If I wear a skirt, she starts saying stuff like it's a problem or something.

A skirt is a symbol of submission to men... You can't climb a tree in a skirt, for example, but you can in trousers

But if you want to climb a tree you just lift up your skirt...

Anyway, here in France, life is okay for women. There are other places much worse, like in the Arabias or whatever (where a man can marry, like, ten women at the same time!).

I saw a TV documentary where the husband was in a Ferrari with ten SUVs behind it (his wives)

But there are still inequalities between men and women, even in France. For example, there's never been a female president...

And there are no "cleaning men"

I'll leave you to clean up my office but don't touch my files!

Yes, Madame President!

But to be honest, I don't mind if a man marries loads of women. It doesn't bother me. Sorry if that offends you, but I'm allowed to think what I want!

I'd happily be one of Ryan Gosling's many wives

He's so good-looking that we'd have to share him (LOL)

But, in return, girls should be able to marry loads of boys too.

Me the president and my husbands! LOL!

Black M   Kendji   Gims

Daniel Balavoine (heart him)

(Based on a true story told by Esther A, who is 12 years old)

Riad Sattouf

The Very Ancient Race

You remember I have an unusual brother called Antoine?

Pssst, Esther! You know about the reptilians?

Like snakes and stuff? Yeah, I know. I hate them

This is him and me in the bedroom we share

Before, he was a punk and wanted to be a rapper, but this year he's more "normal".

Not reptiles! Reptilians!

They're a mysterious race that control the world apparently

Ha ha well yeah...

Look. YouTube.

First I thought it was funny. Then he showed me some YouTube videos and I admit I freaked out (that means "I got really scared" in the language of the street), even if you can tell it's sort of fake.

?

Here's the proof...

The reptilians are supposedly an intelligent species of beings descended from dinosaurs who live underground. They secretly control humans for mysterious reasons.

Us humans come from monkeys

The reptilians come from dinosaurs

They're not extraterrestrials because they're <u>from Earth</u>! I think that's the scary part. Apparently some of them take human form and are famous celebrities exercising power over society.

The Queen of England is an extremely old and powerful reptilian

She NEVER blinks

Intriguing, right?

One of the ways you can recognize them

To spot a reptilian, you have to watch their eyes in the videos. From time to time, their REAL and SERIOUSLY FREAKY eyes become visible for a fraction of a second.

All American presidents are reptilians

That would explain a LOT...

Pointy ears: another sign!

To start with, people believed Obama wasn't one, but in fact he is

Incredible but true: François Hollande is also a reptilian. He looks so nice... but I saw a video where you can see his real eyes.

You see him looking at a toy submarine (weird)

Gasp!

<u>Reptilian eyes</u>

My brother explained that they all know one another and they pretend to be humans to take revenge on us and lead us to our downfall.

The reptilians are a very ancient race who are dying out... They hate humans because they're jealous of us...

Even if it's not true, I adore this kind of stuff: the mysterious secrets of the world, etc. I'd like to read books about that (which is why I dream of being an editor).

Reptilians? Excellent. Lots of potential...

Soon there'll be an election to choose the next French president. Which of them do you think could be reptilians?*

(Based on a true story told by Esther A, who is 12 years old)

Riad Sattouf

* Just kidding — I think they're all humans

137

Politics

Everything has gone well at my new school. I haven't had any problems adapting or mixing with kids from a different social background.

MWAH

This is me kissing my best friend Eva on the cheek to say hello to her in the morning

The people in my class aren't interested in politics at all (except for making fun of Trump).

Eva sometimes writes this on the blackboard before the teacher arrives

OKAY!

HAHA

TRUMP = POO

That makes us laugh

The students know there's an election coming but, well, life goes on.

They're mental

PRESIDEEEENT DON'T-GIVE-A-SHIIIIIIT

Boys shout that sometimes

They mostly talk about how good-looking or ugly the candidates are, because it's important: if they get elected, you'll see them everywhere (so it's better if they're good-looking).

Honestly, I think Fillon looks pretty good

Ugh, whaaaat? You're totally crazy, girl!

Eva always calls me "girl". It's street

I tell you: it's Marine Le Pen. She's fresh.

I kiffe her.

Oh, yeah, girl

I was shocked by this because I don't like Marine Le Pen (you know why, right? If she's elected, we'll have to move to a distant land called Belgium and I don't want to do that!).

Seriously, you want her to be the president?

Yeah, girl, I'm sick of terrorists.

Aren't you?

Eva explained that Marine Le Pen would be extremely harsh on the Islamists or whatever and hunt them down in "ruthless" mode, so she liked her.

But she likes Trump!

But she wants to KILL the terrorists. That's what matters.

Then she showed me a website that calculated each candidate's chances of being elected and Le Pen had, like, a really big score.

Check it out, girl, she's going to win...

What about "Macron"?

Ha ha, nobody even knows who he is

I don't know who Macron is either, or what he wants to do... but since he seems to be the only one who can defeat Marine Le Pen, I like him.

As an idea, I mean

Because, physically, he's not my type at all

Too goody-goody

Could he beat her?

And then Eva told me that her parents were Le Pen supporters and they were going to vote for her!

GASP! No! You have to try to convince them not to! We won't see each other any more if I live in Belgium!

We can write!

ARE YOU SERIOUS, GIRL?!?

(Based on a true story told by Esther A, who is 12 years old)

Riad Sattouf

138

The Pancake

As I get older, I seem to be developing a passion for the world of cuisine.

This is me on holiday at my granny's house watching "Top Chef", a brilliant TV show about cooking

My parents were in Saint-Malo, the town with dogs on the beach

I like the candidates' energy and creativity and the fact that they're all competing against each other and one of them will be the winner.

We're going to make a carrot reduction, which we'll mix with caramel, varying the textures so that there's a combination of crunchiness and smoothness and a satisfying harmony in the mouth

I also love their "pro" way of talking

I'd thought that I wanted to be an editor when I grew up, but now I have this new passion I'm not sure any more...

Granny, can I try to make a meal out of what's in the fridge?

Of course

A half-eaten saucisson, some leftover shop-bought raclette, some Mini Babybel cheese, apricot jam...

All we need is... Hey! PER-FECT.

A pancake almost past its sell-by date

And now I'm just going to give free rein to my creativity!

I rubbed butter on the pancake to liven it up a bit (it was dry and brittle)

Having fun

Then, in one half of the pancake, I sprinkled bits of the raclette and the Babybel cheese

On top I placed a few slices of saucisson for its colour and the play of chaud-froid

Mmm, the smell of hot cheese

In the other half: big spoonfuls of jam

Smells of apricot and springtime

My idea was to have the main course and the dessert on the same pancake (clever, right?)

That looks good, my dear, but sweet-and-savoury is not really my thing

Me in "proud" mode

That suited me! I ate it all and it was delicious (Saucisson and apricot is a surprisingly great combination IMO — you should try it!)

The salty, generous flavour of melted cheese

And the playful sweetness of the jam

Then suddenly I asked:

Who are you going to vote for, Granny?

Well, I was going to vote for Le Pen, but given that your dad says he'll move to Belgium if she wins, I don't know now.

WTF

(Based on a true story told by Esther A, who is 12 years old)

Riad Sattouf

The Illuminati

When I discovered that my grandmother had been planning to vote for Marine Le Pen, I was, like, totally shocked.

This is her and me in "are you serious?" mode.

There are too many foreigners in France and nobody does anything.

I was annoyed

My grandmother lives in Bain-de-Bretagne, in Brittany. She told me that when she came to Paris to see us, some Rebeus spat at her for no reason and ever since then she's been afraid of them and wanted them to go away.

Granny! It's not a Rebeu thing to spit on girls, it's a boy thing!

All boys spit on girls!

That's life!

Thankfully, my dad played his "Belgium" card and my grandmother changed her mind (it's good to be able to change your mind).

I'll vote for Mélenchon then, like your father...

Afterwards, my parents and my brothers came back from their walk and everybody talked politics. We discussed who would face Marine Le Pen in the final vote (because she'll be there no matter what, apparently).

Mélenchon will get through to the second round for sure...

HAHA no way...

Mélenchon wants to take money from the rich and give it to the poor (which is, honestly, the right thing to do, so it's not surprising that my dad likes him – my dad is a good man).

Oh, and you think Hamon will make it?

He'll surprise everyone!

Hamon is a very nice candidate who wants to give money to everybody (not just the poor). I must admit I like him.

I'm sick of the left. I'm just saying it like I see it.

Thanks for that, Mum.

If I were you, I'd vote Macron because he's an Illuminati, yo

And the Illuminati always win

Antoine explained that Macron had worked for "Roz Child" or something, this secret bank that controls the world, and that this was the bank of the Illuminati, a mysterious sect whose symbol is a freaky pyramid with an eye on top – which is also on the dollar!

It's a really scary, mysterious drawing, right?

Italian writing

It really is on dollar bills – shady, don't you think?

That eye gives me the shivers

My dad laughed at him and said he'd rather Antoine believed in the Illuminati than took drugs.

But in fact Mélenchon and Hamon lost, and it was Macron and Le Pen in the final round, just like my brother said!

On the night of the vote, he didn't look surprised

I wish I was an Illuminati...

... you control the world and stuff...

And... Emmanuel Macron comes out in front...

I was impressed

(Based on a true story told by Esther A, who is 12 years old)

Riad Sattouf

140

Ed Sheeran

So I saw part of the debate between Macron and Le Pen on TV.

This is me and my family thinking "That Le Pen woman is off her head"

I mean, when she made those hand movements and said that her voters were hidden here and there, was she serious? I felt sooo sorry for her.

THEY'RE HEEEERE   IN THE COUNTRYSIIIIDE

EVERYWHEEEERE

My evil witch impression

So while we wait for the election to take place, I'm going to talk about a feel-good song that everyone's listening to. That way, if Le Pen is the new president by the time you read this, it'll help you relax a bit.

The song is called "Shape of You"

I think it's about a girl's body.

And the singer is called Aide Shiranne (although he spells it Ed Sheeran)

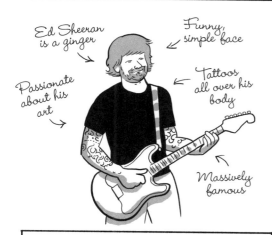

Ed Sheeran is a ginger

Funny, simple face

Tattoos all over his body

Passionate about his art

Massively famous

I don't usually like gingers, I must admit, because looking at their reddish-orange hair gets repetitive after a while.

I don't feel the same way about other hair colours

I'm so glad I'm not a ginger

Unfair, I know

Sorry gingers (LOL)

The video for the song is really good IMO. It starts with Ed Sheeran going to the gym.

A lone wolf

Crazy about boxing

And then he sees this ultra-beautiful Asian-Renoi who's training for some kind of combat sport, in "independent" mode

She does this and Ed Sheeran is impressed by her bendiness

Yep, I can do it too

Afterwards she hits a punchbag

Then she accidentally hurts him by opening the door of his changing room (clumsy) and that's how they meet (romantic).

Warning: cuteness overdose (LOL)

So they go to a restaurant and he orders this enormous plate of chicken or something and he's in "I'm starving after all that sport" mode. It's really funny.

They become friends and then they fall in love, united by their shared passion for sport

---

Then there's this totally crazy part where Ed Sheeran puts on this "fat-man" costume and he has to fight this obese Asian guy who's called a Zulu wrestler or something.

He gets destroyed – so funny

This is him!

And at the end, the Asian-Renoi girl attacks the Zulu to save her beloved Ed. Moral: love is a combat sport and you have to both be warriors to survive.

Warrior girl saving her lover

All Ed Sheeran's videos get, like, a billion views on YouTube (he's the most famous man on the planet). But when I mentioned him to my dad:

I am in love with the shape of you la la

Aide Shiranne? Never heard of him. Is he well known?

Crazy, right? My poor sweet daddy is totally disconnected from reality!

(Based on a true story told by Esther A, who is 12 years old)

141

The Illuminettes

I was soooo relieved this week! I bet you were too!

This is me when I found out we wouldn't have to move to Belgium (as my dad threatened to do if Le Pen won.)

YEEEEAAAAH

And Emmanuel Macron is the new president of

Then Macron gave a speech in front of a pyramid in the Louvre in "I'm the boss" mode.

My brother

Macron

Whoa, shady!

Together for France!

Don't you get it, yo? Macron in front of the pyramid?

The eye at the top of the pyramid!

? ?

GAAASP! THAT THING YOU WERE TALKING ABOUT! THE ILLUMINETTES!

And then my whole family burst out laughing (because I said "Illuminettes" instead of "Illuminati").

HA HA HA HA HA HA

My brother was annoyed because nobody was listening to him now

Whaaaat? Ha ha

The Illuminati are these people who secretly control the world and their symbol is a pyramid with an eye on top. Antoine had told us all that Macron was one of them.

After his speech in front of the pyramid, everyone started saying "Hey, Macron's an Illuminati...

My brother the visionary

Nobody ever listens to me, it pisses me off

After that, I had an idea for a series of YA mystery/comedy novels called "The Illuminettes" (which could also be made into a TV series).

At a prestigious secondary school in Paris, Milena, the most popular student, disappears.

So then a very pretty girl called Carla (I really like that name) becomes the new most popular girl in the school.

Carla, will you come to my birthday party?

Carla!

Carla! I love you

A modest girl, she's not at ease with her new position, but she has to deal with it

Aren't her clothes beautiful?

That evening, she receives a letter marked with a black pyramid, announcing that — as the most popular girl in her school — she is now an Illuminette, a girl who has many powers over other people.

SECRET

Congratulations, you are now an Illuminette but your life is in grave danger...

She discovers that there's an Illuminette in each school, controlling her "people" of submissive girls, and that there's a ruthless war among the Illuminettes...

Pretty girl

Pulling strings

For their own good

Girls doing what they can

... and the Illuminos, the popular boys, who also have a secret organization and want to control the world!

Carla has to investigate them, taking terrible risks...

Careful you don't go too far, Carla...

?!

What do you think? I'd like to be a chef or an editor when I'm older. I like using the mysteries of life to imagine the beginnings of stories...

If anyone wants to write the rest, my idea is for sale: one billion euros please

Joke

(Based on a true story told by Esther A, who is 12 years old)

Riad Sattouf

Rebellion

I haven't got into too much trouble in my life. Even if I'm often tempted to break the rules, I usually don't dare. To be honest I'm often too scared.

This is me on the bus — I haven't swiped my ticket, but I'm staying close to the machine in case a ticket inspector comes along, so I can swipe it at the last minute

When I was in Year 1, I'd ask the teacher if I could go to the toilet, she'd say yes, and I'd go downstairs and just walk straight past the girls' bathroom. I was really scared.

But I couldn't help myself!

I would challenge myself to go a bit farther each time: the end of the corridor, the headmaster's door, all the way to the street!

HEY YOU!

I was relieved that he stopped me before the worst could happen

One day in Year 4, I was late to school and the others were already in class. But instead of going into the classroom, I walked through the corridors and explored the school.

Again, I couldn't help myself

In "crazy" mode

And again, I was stopped before I could open a mysterious wooden door at the end of a corridor.

What was behind it? Another world? (LOL)

Let me see... what else? I cut up an umbrella with scissors once because I was bored.

At home, in "I don't give a shit" mode

In Year 5 I had loads of lovers so I wrote romantic messages on the wall of my bedroom.

My mum really shouted at me afterwards

E + M = ♥
E + L
E + T = ♥♥
E + N = ♥

Oh, and then there was the shoplifting. One day, I tried on a scarf in a shop and then walked out still wearing it. But the alarm went off!

Wiiiii Wiii Wiii

"Oh, sorry!"

"I forgot to take it off"

I'm a good actress when I'm scared

I also had a friend called Eugenie who was SOOOO rich. I often stole nail varnish from her (she had loads of different colours that she never used).

OOOH this video of TAL is soo good

Oh yeah?

But I must admit that the worst thing I ever did wasn't very long ago. I spat at some old lady from my window.

The temptation was too strong

I didn't really think it would hit her

Afterwards I had a panic attack: what if someone had filmed me? And if I was arrested or something? Why did I do that to some poor old lady? She could have been my grandmother!

Esther, how could you?

Sorry Dad

I wanted to apologize to her but it was too late, so I cried all night instead.

Rebellion really isn't my thing

(Based on a true story told by Esther A, who is 12 years old)

Riad Sattouf

143

The Terrorist Attack

At my secondary school, there's a different teacher for each subject (not like primary school, where there's just one teacher). I think it's better this way. I like seeing different faces.

This is me just before a biology test

The (very old) teacher

The other day, something traumatic happened. Honestly, it was terrible.

"Diversity, relatedness and unity of living beings. Answer true or false:
1. A male green frog can reproduce with a female red frog..."

Hmm, that should work...

So anyway, we were in the middle of a test and suddenly this really weird alarm went off.

WEEEEEEEEEEE

And the teacher just started acting... well, weird.

WEEEEEEEEEEE

I... um... Wait... What's... Um...

And then Cassiopée (the best student in the class) said:

That's not the fire alarm, it's a military alarm! It means the school's being attacked!

Then the teacher freaked out and started screaming.

EVERYBODY UNDER THE TABLES! EVERYBODY UNDER THE TABLES! TERRORIST ATTACK!

And then it was just total panic. We all cowered under the tables. The alarm kept wailing...

WEEE

I didn't understand what was going on. I was thinking "There's not really a terrorist attack, is there? This isn't actually happening..."

Eva, a good friend of mine, lost it completely (I was, like, in a dream or something)...

EEEE

It's happening, girl, it's happening

Some boys (the feminists) were crying. A "feminist boy" is one who admits being weak, not tough, and who hangs around with girls.

WEEEEEE

I'm too young to die I'm too young to die

On my father's life, he really said that

Of course the insensitive boys just laughed, in "who gives a shit" mode.

WEEEE

WEEEEE

Some of them played with their fidget spinners and said stuff like

Who gives a flying fuck? It's just a stupid exercise

After a while, I heard the sound of students in the courtyard, so I said:

Miss! I think we have to go outside! Everybody else is out there!

Our saviour (LOL)

I... Yes! OUTSIDE! EVERYBODY OUT!

(Based on a true story told by Esther A, who is 12 years old)

Riad Sattouf

144

The Alarm

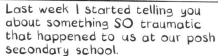

Last week I started telling you about something SO traumatic that happened to us at our posh secondary school.

WEEE WEEEEE

This is me and my classmates evacuating the building because of the alarm!

We all found ourselves in the courtyard and it was totally packed with the entire school in there.

WEEEEE WEEEE

Everybody was talking and stuff

It was like a concert or something

Then the headmaster spoke into a megaphone (this thing that makes your voice louder) and he said:

Silence! You're making far too much noise! The terrorists can hear you! YOU'RE ALL DEAD NOW!

Afterwards, he asked for four minutes' silence and the students shut up a bit. Then Eva pointed out a loudspeaker in the courtyard.

Imagine if a voice came out of that and said "Dear students, the terrorists are coming to kill you. Don't move."

AND THEN SUDDENLY, ON MY MOTHER'S LIFE...

DEAR STUDENTS...

GASP!

... please walk calmly back to your classrooms. The evacuation exercise is over.

We went back to the classroom and then the teacher did this weird performance where she acted like we'd all forgotten that she'd totally lost it, thinking that there really WAS a terrorist attack instead of understanding that it was just an exercise.

Well, I have something to tell you all. I'm sorry, but...

... if there really was a terrorist attack, it would make no difference how you reacted. You would all die anyway.

SERIOUSLY, THAT'S WHAT SHE SAID!

Us in "um, WHAT did she say?" mode

If there's an attack and you find yourself face to face with a terrorist, I would advise you to do nothing. Don't move.

Everyone who's ever tried to run away or talk them out of it... they've all died.

With no exceptions.

So perhaps if you do nothing and just look at them without moving, they won't do anything?

Help me, I'm in shock... is she really saying this to children?

It's worth a try

(Based on a true story told by Esther A, who is 12 years old)

Riad Sattouf

145

Flying

The other day, everyone in my family was asleep and I snuck out into the street, in "I'm free" mode.

This is me thinking how weird it is that there's nobody else around

Then I discovered that if I jumped in the air and made a breaststroke movement...

I would hover above the ground

I started swimming through the air and flew up over the rooftops!

Strange they never told us we could do this at school!

Suddenly I saw a sort of gigantic church in the distance.

Weird... I never knew that existed!

A light at the top!

A restaurant! I think I'll stop there for a rest!

Restaurant

Good evening, miss. Please take a seat. We were expecting you.

Thank you, my good man.

I sat down in "there's a restaurant at the top of a huge church AND they were expecting me?!?" mode.

Only flyers can eat here, you see...

Ah. I see.

And then he brought me this enormous strawberry Tagada (just my favourite sweet in the whole world!)

I took a bite and it wasn't sweet at all — it was warm and slightly salty

But I ate it anyway LOL

It was a dream, of course, not reality. (I REALLY wish I could find out if any readers believed me when they read the first few panels! That would be sooo funny!)

The next morning, I tried to do the flying breaststroke

I'm crazy

Well, you never know! It could have been us humans' secret gift and nobody had ever tried!

(Based on a true story told by Esther A, who is 12 years old)

146

The Wound

Something tragic happened this week that really made me grow up. I learned two important things: 1. Just because you love something doesn't mean it loves you back, and 2. You should never underestimate the call of the wild. As you know, I have a Russian hamster called Manuela, and I really loved her (like a big sister or something). So, the other day, I wanted to take her out of her cage and give her a hug. I really thought she'd be pleased — that it would make her happy. So anyway, I opened the cage to pick her up...

(Based on a true story told by Esther A, who is 12 years old)

Riad Sattouf

Money

When I was little, I used to love money.

This is me in "but today I don't give a shit" mode

HAHA! MONEY!

WHO NEEDS IT?

This cartoon panel is a joke — in real life I don't throw money away

---

Money is something that's used to buy stuff. But unlike food or drink, money is not necessary to life.

For example, you can live in the wild without money

Berries to eat

River water to drink

But since human beings are lazy, they use money to make life simple.

Bottle of Cristaline bought with money

GLUG GLUG GLUG

Strawberries from the supermarket

The first time I had money, it was the tooth fairy who gave it to me.

I got 1 euro in exchange for my tooth!

The first thing I bought with money was a farty rubber pig.

PFRRRT

It made this noise when you pressed on it (hilarious)

I never asked my parents for money. I didn't want to be a burden on them... But one day, my dad said:

Esther, sweetheart! I'd like to give you some pocket money every month. So you can learn to manage cash.

Huh? Naah, there's no need

But my dad insisted, so to make him happy I accepted.

We agreed on the sum of 5 euros

Every month I get a piece of paper with a number 5 on it (LOL)

Since I don't know what else to do with it, I buy gifts for my parents to thank them for looking after me since my birth.

I gave my beloved father a necklace with a "wolf" charm that symbolizes "family"

For my mum, the same but with a hummingbird to symbolize "happiness"

I didn't give anything to my little brother (too young) or to my brother Antoine.

Besides, I couldn't find an animal to symbolize stupidity...

(Just kidding! He's actually less stupid now that he's interested in conspiracy theories)

For the first time, a video shows the reality of the Bohemian Club, the most evil secret society of all time

Whoa... fuuuck

The two necklaces cost me 15 euros (yep, you read that right: three months of pocket money)!

What can I say? I adore my parents!

At school, though, I'm pretty much the exception.

5 euros? Are you kidding, girl? How do you manage?

I get 500 euros a month and I can hardly make ends meet...

My friend Eva

Yes, that's right, we're in Year 7

(Based on a true story told by Esther A, who is 12 years old)

Riad Sattouf

148

Wealth

This year, I'm in Year 7 at a public (that means free) secondary school in the centre of Paris (which means there are loads of rich kids, because you have to be wealthy to live there).

This is me, shocked to discover that Eva gets 500 euros a month in pocket money

GASP! Will you show me?

I get 5 euros

Every month she gets the equivalent of 8 years of pocket money for me.

I'd be 20 before I got that much!

I can't girl, it's in the bank

What can she possibly do with all that money? I wouldn't have a clue how to spend it.

With 500 euros, you could buy 1,000 "Head Bangers"

They're sour sweets

That's more than a lifetime supply!

Some months I go crazy and spend it all on clothes and gadgets...

And I'm broke by the 20th...

Other times I do my little banker act – I spend nothing and at the end of 3 months I have 1,500 euros, yo.

So funny!

I'd never tell her this but I'm shocked that children get paid so much. When I think about all the poor people in the world eating nothing but twigs...

... I could almost weep

When I'm a grown-up, though, I'd like to be very rich and have at least 20,000 euros (with that much, you probably wouldn't have to worry about anything).

10 a.m.... No need to get up – I've got 20,000 euros in my bank account...

Maître Gims and Black M are VERY rich, of course. Fame and fortune go hand in hand.

I bet they've got at least a million each

The singer Adele is one of the richest women in the world. Apparently she's got billions (although I don't listen to her music).

She deserves it

My parents aren't rich. I would guess they've got about 2,000 euros?

My dad really hates the rich – it's hilarious

DO YOU REALLY NEED YOUR BIG FAT TURBO SUV IN PARIS, YOU PRICK?!

Oh stop being an old man, yo... You'd love it if you were rich...

NOT AT ALL

Antoine my crazy brother

You're JEALOUS of the rich, just like all POOR PEOPLE

WHAT?!

Watch the road

(Based on a true story told by Esther A, who is 12 years old)

Riad Sattouf

The Power of Analytical Thinking

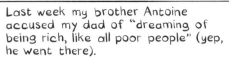

Last week my brother Antoine accused my dad of "dreaming of being rich, like all poor people" (yep, he went there).

This is me watching my dad fume because he hates the rich

My mum laughing

HaHa

I'd rather not answer that...

For a while now, Antoine has loved having debates with my dad (he always thinks the exact opposite of him).

If you had millions, you wouldn't want the poor to take it from you. You'd be just like all rich people...

HA HA!

Nah, but you're not being logical, you know... You moan about the rich and that, but you did everything you could to make sure Esther went to a posh school...

For the quality of the teaching, not the social class

Pfft

Okay, and if "the quality of the teaching" helps Esther succeed and become mega-rich, what will you do? Hate her?

Naaah...

My brother gets on my nerves but he's not always wrong. It's true that my dad would like to be rich (but he doesn't want to admit it).

... because you don't just hope that she'll become rich...

He knows that he'll never get rich working in a gym, so hating the rich is a way of venting his frustration.

... you hope that she'll GIVE YOU MONEY! That's why you want her to be educated!

I feel sorry for my poor dad. It hurts him.

Antoine, I preferred it when you banged on about Nekfeu or the Illuminati

Sarcasm... Because you've been outwitted by my powers of analytical thinking, yo! Ha ha out-WIT-ted!

HEY, STOP HAVING A GO AT HIM!

Yes, I want to be, like, MEGA-RICH and yes, I'll GIVE ALL MY MONEY TO DAD!

So what? What're you gonna do about it?

Nothing!

The powers of analytical thiiiiinkiiiing!

He's right!

(Based on a true story told by Esther A, who is 12 years old)

Riad Sattouf

The Horror Story

The other night I had a sleepover at Cassandra's house. She was my best friend in primary school and now she's at a private secondary school and her dad died when we were in Year 5 and... You remember who she is, right? Anyway...

This is me and her in the same bed in "trying to freak each other out with horror stories" mode

Listen to this. It's a true story...

One day, when she was a child, my aunt went to an antiques dealer with her father. And there, in a window display, she saw...

Daddy, look! What a pretty doll! I want it!

The old saleswoman, who looked like a skeleton, said: "That's the tic-tac doll, young lady, and she's not for sale."

Couldn't we come to an agreement? Here's 1,000 euros

The rich father managed to convince the old lady. But as they were leaving...

Watch out! At night, you must lock the tic-tac doll in a cupboard! If you don't... SOMETHING TERRIBLE WILL HAPPEN!

Yeah okay, bye!

Back at home, my aunt played with the doll then put it in a cupboard in the basement.

No need to lock it...

She went to bed and fell asleep. But suddenly, in the middle of the night, she heard:

TIC-TAC TIC-TAC I'M IN THE CUPBOARD

TIC-TAC TIC-TAC I'M OUT OF THE CUPBOARD

TIC-TAC TIC-TAC I'M IN THE HALLWAY

TIC-TAC TIC-TAC I'M OUTSIDE YOUR DOOR

TIC-TAC-TIC-TAC I'M GOING TO KILL YOU

TIC-TAC-TIC

BOOO!

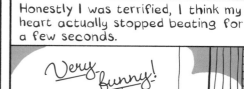

Honestly I was terrified, I think my heart actually stopped beating for a few seconds.

Very funny!

It's weird how I like being scared

(Based on a true story told by Esther A, who is 12 years old)

Riad Sattouf

Areas with Major Constraints

This year, one of the things I learned that's stayed with me was about "areas with major constraints".

This is me laughing because you don't know what that means. I'm right, aren't I?

In fact they're places where people live that have lots of constraints, making life there more difficult than where we live.

I was very moved by this because I put myself in those people's place

Seriously, it made my head spin

For a start, there are HOT DESERTS. Terribly high temperatures, no water or hospitals, few towns, living in tents...

Esther! Quick, get some water from the well — your mother has a fever

OKAY DAD!

Of course the well is soooooooooo far away (12.4 miles, in fact) and I'm the only one who can go there. And then I have to come back.

Pressure

Next, there are COLD DESERTS (North and South Pole, Siberia, tundra...)

OMG I would hate to live there

I always feel cold even in Paris

And then there are all the animals constantly attacking us because they're cold and hungry too...

After that, there are HIGH MOUNTAINS, where it's impossible to build roads or have electricity and the air's too thin to breathe...

And apparently if you live there too long you gradually become shorter

And SMALL ISLANDS: people think they're paradise because the weather's good but there's nothing to do so you're totally bored...

Sigh

It made me realize how lucky I was to be born, by pure chance, in Paris. Thank you, chance!

At the same time, I share my bedroom with my brother Antoine who listens to PNL at top volume on his headphones (PNL is a rap group formed by drug dealers but I don't understand any of the words).

UM HELLO?! UM UM HELLO?!

In fact MY BEDROOM is an area of major constraints (LOL)

I LEAVE TRACES OF E IN THE WC TOTALLY DESTROYED IN THE LV I COMEBACK POCKETS FULL OF COKE

?!

(Based on a true story told by Esther A, who is 12 years old)

Riad Sattouf

Writing

I started writing a novel this week (reading is one of my passions). I'm just trying to see if I can do it (I want to be an editor when I grow up).

This is me possessed by the demon of inspiration (LMAO)

I like stories where the narrator says "I", you know, where it's like someone telling their story in "diary" mode... I don't like it so much when "she" does this or that.

That's why I like "Esther's Notebooks" (just kidding)

I also like mystery, horror, action, monsters and anything romantic.

The title of my book is: "Memoirs of a Teenage Vampire".

Mysterious, right?

In fact, I imagined what would happen if I became a vampire. In a totally realistic way. It all starts one night when I'm alone at home...

Doing my homework...

Suddenly I hear a child crying outside...

Opening the window

Waah heeelp

Waaaaaah

And then... OMG! A little girl is hanging on the window ledge. If she falls, she could die!

Help me, I beg you! Let me inside!

I'm going to fall

Because I'm gentle and compassionate, I help her and invite her into my bedroom... BIG MISTAKE!

It'll be okay, little girl! What are your parents called?

Waah

Her eyes are so blue and so deep... I look into them and I'm spellbound...

You were nice to me so I won't kill you now... In fact, I'm going to give you a beautiful gift...

The next morning I wake up with the vague memory of a strange, scary dream...

My brother is in bed. I didn't hear my family come home

Rhh

In the kitchen my parents are eating breakfast...

Morning, Esther!

Oh sweetie, you've got acne... There are two spots on your neck...

I run to the bathroom.

(Based on a true story told by Esther A, who is 12 years old)

Riad Sattouf

153

The Icy Wind

I think I like writing my book. Even if it's pretty exhausting.

This is me rereading the first 10 pages →

← Serious stuff

In last week's episode: after helping a little vampire girl, I was bitten by her. What will happen now?

This scarf should be perfect for hiding the teeth marks...

I can still see myself in the mirror...

← ...so everything's okay

I go to school as normal. I feel kind of floaty...

The light hurts my eyes a little, but it's not a problem...

.... I have my heart-shaped sunglasses

Yeah, it's raining. So what? →

I don't take them off in the classroom. The teacher says something about this. "The light hurts me, I'm keeping them on," I say in an echoey voice that frightens the old lady.

Oh... Ok-k-Kay Esther, as you like...

At lunch in the cafeteria, the food makes me feel sick... but no more than normal...

Um... Are you sure you're okay, girl? You look kinda weird

Yeah... I just hate these vegetables

I love the colour of your sweater though.

At the end of the day, some bad boys from Year 10 insult me for no reason as usual.

Hey, give us those sunglasses, ho

Before I even realize what's happening, his throat is pulsating in my hands. He suffocates like a fish out of water.

You've... already... got... glasses... dickhead

Disturbing little voice →

Ach

Scared by my own strength, I vanish like a shadow while the ambulance sirens scream...

A pleasantly icy wind sweeps me away

At home, I feel refreshed by the dusk, and as soon as the sun goes down I'm filled with energy.

Hello sweetie ...

My dad coming home from work →

What a beautiful daughter I have! You just get prettier every day...

MWAH

(Based on a true story told by Esther A, who is 12 years old)

Riad Sattouf

The Murder

I'm making good progress on my book about vampires!

This is me in "counting the pages again" mode

I've already written 12 pages!

Not bad, right?

In last week's episode: one day after being bitten, I notice the first changes in my body and I'm shocked.

After almost biting my father, I ran to my bedroom before I could do something unforgivable

I tell him I'm feeling ill so I can stay under the covers.

Do you want something to eat? Shall I call a doctor?

NO, DON'T CALL! I'm... I'm fine, I just need to rest!

Now get out and LEAVE ME ALONE!

When everybody is asleep, I'm lured into the night.

I'm starving, so I jump out the window in "this seems normal" mode

Ow, I bit my lip when I hit the ground

GASP!

At that moment, I see the building's concierge staring at me from the hallway.

Weird but true: that ugly woman looks as delicious to me as a four-cheese pizza!

I kill her because I'm still a beginner vampire (yeah, I like horror when it's funny) and the blood gets everywhere.

I come back to myself and start worrying about the consequences of my act, which has covered the hall in blood.

GASP but... but... what will my parents think when they find out that I...

Who cares? Why does it matter if they find out? You're not one of them any more...

THE LITTLE VAMPIRE GIRL WHO CREATED ME!

Look what a mess you made! I'm going to have to teach you...

...MY DAUGHTER.

(Based on a true story told by Esther A, who is 12 years old)

Riad Sattouf

The Difficulty of Writing

Writing is really hard. It requires imagination and motivation. I know because I started writing a book...

... and it's really really difficult to stay concentrated and control everything.

Plus, writing a horror story like this gets you thinking about weird stuff that you wouldn't normally think about...

For example, if you're a vampire, that means you're dead, cursed and... __eternal__.

But being eternal also means watching all your "non-vampire" loved ones die.

Not only that, but you're watching your loved ones die while desperately wanting to suck all their blood!

Then I thought of a less tragic solution: I could turn my whole family into vampires to keep them close to me.

Even my little brother who would be, like, the youngest vampire ever.

And then imagining my brother Antoine as a vampire annoying me for eternity... that was annoying

I even imagined that I'd visit President Macron and turn him into a vampire (crazy idea, right?)

There are so many possibilities when you're writing, and you have to make all these choices...

... I think I'll stick to being a reader and an editor.

(Based on a true story told by Esther A, who is 12 years old)

Riad Sattouf

Shame

Year 7 is over, so Eva and I organized a party to celebrate!

This is me and my dad, who's congratulating me on my school report (yep, I did well)

Look how happy he is!

We invited almost the whole class to Luxembourg (it's a public garden near our school) for a "party"-style picnic.

We went shopping (juice, sweets, etc.)

Get some Innocent

Oh yeah!

We sat on the grass in the sun. It was sooo nice.

And suddenly one of the boys started throwing water at another boy...

... and it turned into this massive water fight!!!

After a while, three boys poured WHOLE BOTTLES of water on me!

How we laughed

When suddenly...

?

HEY... ?

We'd moved away from our bags and some guy was rummaging through them!

THAT'S OURS! THAT'S OURS!

And then he started yelling at us that he hated us and that rich kids like us were the worst people in the world or something...

Plus loads of swear words that grown-ups don't normally say to children

So anyway we shouted at him and in the end he went away. Nobody came to help us!

Fuck you! Fuck you all!

We just wanted him to stop going through our stuff — what's wrong with him?

That was when I noticed that everyone in the park was looking at ME

The water had made my dress transparent

(Based on a true story told by Esther A, who is 12 years old)

Riad Sattouf

157

The African Dream

The other night I dreamed of Africa (this really beautiful place that I hope to visit one day).

This is me walking through the savannah in "no worries" mode

I'm not afraid of lions or tigers. I know nothing can happen to me here because the animals of the savannah respect me.

Suddenly in the distance I see an unfamiliar shape...

HA HA HA
IT'S GOT A MAN'S EARS!

HA HA! I DON'T BELIEVE IT!

I'm laughing hysterically. I want to tell the elephant I'm sorry, that I can't help it, but it's impossible because I'm laughing too hard... So it gets REALLY ANNOYED and storms off.

HANG ON, I...
BAHAHAHAHAA

And I woke up laughing!

HAHA

FUNNY, RIGHT?

(Based on a true story told by Esther A, who is 12 years old)

Riad Sattouf

158

The Romani

Do you know about the Romani?

This is me with my dad in the street, looking at them

They're poor vagrants with no country who beg and sleep on the streets of our cities.

I could easily be her (sad face)

Why doesn't anybody help them (government, president or whatever)? Can someone answer me?

The other day, Cassandra and me went out in "old friends reunited" mode

She's doing fine actually

We walked past a group of Romani sitting on the ground and a boy looked at us. He was very good-looking.

Dark eyes

He even had stylish clothes

I smiled at him!

AND THEN... WELL, HE STARTED FOLLOWING US!

Umm, we have a problem, Esther

I turned around and he smiled at me.

He had a sparkling smile, literally: one of his teeth was gold!

Cassandra totally freaked. Apparently she's scared of Romani people so she shouted "Run!"

He's going to kidnap us!

And when we turned around again...

He was still there! On my mother's life, he'd run after us.

I'M SCARED!

So we went into a bakery...

Then he disappeared

What did he want? Why did he scare us after I'd smiled at him? Did he think I was making fun of him? Or what if we were wrong about all of it?

I regretted running, I admit

What if he felt rejected? Poor Romani people! The French government should give them their own département, so that could be their country.

Like the Auvergne, maybe?

Apparently nobody lives there

They could call it Romie? Or Romania (but wait, that already exists). Or even Romance! Or another name...

I think that would be nice for them

(Based on a true story told by Esther A, who is 12 years old)

Riad Sattouf

Kisses

Do you like kisses? I do.

This is me kissing my wrist so I can feel what other people feel when I kiss them

Have you noticed that it's possible to analyse someone's personality by the way they kiss?

A kiss is when your mouth turns into a little suction pad and makes a sort of wet sound

MMWAH!

Everybody on this planet should kiss each other instead of fighting, don't you think? (I make myself laugh like crazy when I say that kind of thing).

Apparently you have to kiss at least four people a day to be happy

Myth or reality?

For example, my dad's kisses (which I adore).

A series of very quick kisses

Mwah mwah mwah mwah

It's a technique to get in lots of kisses in the time normally reserved for just one kiss.

Mwah mwah mwah mwah

Clever

Personality: enjoys life 150%

I like my mum's kisses too. They're like little mouth tickles. They make me laugh.

She attacks by surprise

Personality: mischievous (yep, that's her)

I'm trying to train my little brother to kiss. Impossible. He won't even try and that GETS ON MY NERVES!

DO IT — ON MY CHEEK!

WAAAH

Personality: rebellious and impossible

My brother Antoine has NEVER kissed me. Like, NOT ONCE. Incredible, right?

Personality: weird and annoying

My friends kiss me a lot. Eva always keeps her mouth slightly open, for example.

Mwah hha!

Personality: insecure about air — needs to breathe a lot

Cassandra stops moving completely when she kisses. It's the kissee (new word alert LOL) who ends the kiss, not her!

If I don't move away, she just stays like that

Personality: affectionate and maybe a little clingy

I don't really know how to analyse my kisses. I'd say that only my lips move and I never close my eyes.

Mwwah

What do you think?

(Based on a true story told by Esther A, who is 12 years old)

Riad Sattouf

160

Safety

I love feeling safe. And the place I feel the safest on earth is in my bed, under my covers. I curl up inside them, leaving just a little hole that I can breathe through. It's warm and cosy in my hiding place. I feel so good there and I imagine all sorts of harsh, freaky things happening outside that can't reach me (and that makes me even happier to be where I am)... For example:

A storm is blowing, rain pours down, the air is cold, and death prowls in a hostile landscape... ...but none of it touches me

A river of lava flows endlessly, wiping out all life... ...but my shelter is spared from the magma

I'm at the bottom of the ocean... ...in my bubble

I've gone billions of years back in time and I'm surrounded by vicious dinosaurs... ROARRr ...but my shelter keeps them away!

I'm on an ice floe and it's so cold that even the penguins are freezing... WOUUUUUUUU ...but I'm perfectly warm (ha ha)

I'm on a little platform at the top of a pylon that rises above the clouds, thousands of feet in the air... ...but my eyes are closed, so I don't get vertigo

I'm on the moon, and everybody else is far, far away... ...and I feel fine

Now I just have to fall asleep (LOL)

(Based on a true story told by Esther A, who is 12 years old)

Riad Sattouf

161

Gaëtan

You probably remember that I have a little brother. His name is Gaëtan and he'll be 2 in November.

This is him and me in "perfect big sister" mode

I'm reading him a story

I like watching him grow up. It's very interesting to see all the things that make us different, even at such a young age.

... Kaki says "Whyyyy do I have to sleep?"

Gaëtan.

HUH?

VVRRRTCHH

I'm trying to awaken his "feminine" side (sensitivity, gentleness, understanding) and believe me it's hard.

Gaëtan, can you please stay focused? If you can't focus, you'll never get anywhere in life! I'M READING YOU A STORY HERE.

VRRCHH!

BIN LOWWY!

VVRRCHIIIVRRR

Total fascination →

I think boys must be born with different interests.

BIIIN LOOOOWWY!

VVRRCHIIIH!

Personally, I couldn't give a flying fuck about bin lorries... When I was a kid, it was all dolls and girly stuff.

I gave life to these plastic objects using my imagination

BAY-BEE

I had a Nenuco, I remember

So I knew from a very young age that I'd be a mother one day (I want four daughters).

I never got rid of it!

Gaëtan! Come over here, we're going to look after the little baby. He needs his diaper changing and...

NO!

Gaëtan will probably be a binman. You can't argue with destiny.

Bin lowwy

VRRCHHH!

We're born girls or boys, with our similarities but also our differences. Let's just try to get along!

Come on Nenuco, let's drive this BIN LORRY

vroum vroum

Bin lowwy?

NO!

And let's accept that this situation will never change.

La La La

(Based on a true story told by Esther A, who is 12 years old)

Riad Sattouf

Esther's Notebooks: the Film

Listen up, this is totally fresh yo! I recently found out that some film producers (very rich people who make and pay for films) were interested in turning the cartoon books of "Esther's Notebooks" into a film with real actors and everything!!! INCREDIBLE, right? But please <u>please</u> don't cast French actors because they're rubbish. You need to get Americans — they're way more talented. Okay? And whatever you do, you have to get adult actors to play all the roles, even us young ones, because it's easier to identify with them. So here are a few suggestions for the cast (well, you never know).

<u>My dad: Johnny Depp</u>

I like this actor because he's funny and good-looking (yep, just like my dad) and he even looks like him

Passionate and tender

<u>My mum: Gal Gadot</u>

She's the one who played Wonder Woman. A dynamic woman who's not afraid of going out in public without make-up, and who used to be a model

<u>My little brother:</u> Just find a child model with a sweet angelic face (there aren't any 2-year-old celebrities)

The three boys fighting over me: <u>Matthew Morrison</u>: Looks good enough to eat (LOL)

<u>Antoine:</u> <u>Nekfeu</u> The only French guy in the cast (my brother's a huge fan so this is for him)

<u>Chace Crawford:</u> ♡

<u>My friend Eva:</u> <u>Jayma Mays</u> Sarcastic redhead, not too pretty

Me: <u>Cara Delevingne</u> Actress, model, melancholic... I adore her!

<u>An enemy:</u> <u>Mercedes Lambre</u> from "Violetta": She's beautiful and horrible at the same time

<u>Chris Pine</u>: Casually bewitching, darkly handsome blond

<u>Not bad, huh?</u>

(Based on a true story told by Esther A, who is 12 years old)

Riad Sattouf

163

Nostalgia

Um, you might want to sit down for this. I'm going to tell you something that will probably shock you.

This is me going to buy bread and anticipating your reaction

I LOVE THE FIRST DAY OF SCHOOL!

Yep, I'm not like everybody else!

I like the ATMOSPHERE of this time of year.

It's usually overcast and raining: autumn is coming

I'm full of nostalgic thoughts, as if someone had their hand round my heart and was squeezing really hard.

I think about all the time that's gone past and will never come back, in "I'm getting older" mode...

... and about everything that might happen to me this year and also during the rest of my life.

wouuu

I didn't go to summer camp this year (they were fully booked), so I stayed at my granny's house in Brittany.

It was autumn all summer long, I swear

I did my summer schoolwork – I love that!

Maybe I sound like a nerd or something but I don't care

"The unity of the city of Athens had three aspects: religious, political and military..."

Ah yes, that's true

I don't know what Year 8 will be like!

I can't wait to see my new teachers and their new faces

I'd really like to be the best student in my school to make my parents proud...

I love them soooo much

... without losing my reputation as someone adorably funny and likeable, of course!

Me and my friends in "side-splitting" mode

I'd like to continue being loved by everybody.

That's not too much to ask, is it?

(Based on a true story told by Esther A, who is 12 years old)

Riad Sattouf

164

Today was the first day of school — and it was very strange.

This is me waking up at 10:20 a.m. (yep, you read that right)

YAWN...

After that I vegged out at home (breakfast, TV, then a nap, as if I hadn't already slept enough).

True love will find you...

My parents were at work, Antoine was at school, Gaëtan was with his childminder...

And here's me, the girl who doesn't give a...

SNCF, let's get together

I texted with Eva and we arranged to meet up outside the school at 2 p.m. ...

Because, yep, the first day of school began at THREE O'CLOCK!

- hey whassup
- sup
- meet u outsd skool ok?

fresh yo!

Around 11:30 I took a shower and as I stared at the tiles on the wall...

In "groggy" mode

... I swear it really felt like I was a FROG.

Hel-looo wild girl

After that, my mum suggested we eat lunch at a restaurant near the school.

I met her, looking totally natural

Zero make-up

No special "first day of school" outfit

The food was good but too peppery. My mouth was on fire.

We had a laugh

I walked from the restaurant to my school and this really good-looking adult man smiled at me in the street.

So he doesn't give a shit that I'm 12 or what?

Creepy

Then we all stood in the school courtyard and the headmistress gave a really boring speech.

... and let me be clear: I don't want to see any more sweet wrappers in the courtyard this year...

So here's something new: there are going to be two types of class representatives this year: "normal reps" and "green reps" who have to look after trees and tell the caretaker when the bins are full.

Me and my friends all want to be representatives!

Nah I'm joking (LMFAO)

This is the weirdest first day of school ever!

Pfrrrt!

Harf!

(Based on a true story told by Esther A, who is 12 years old)

Riad Sattouf

A Note About the Author

Riad Sattouf is a best-selling cartoonist, comic artist, and filmmaker who was born in France, spent his childhood in Libya and Syria, and now lives in Paris. His graphic memoir *The Arab of the Future* has sold more than three million copies in France and has been translated into twenty-three languages. Originally published in France, *Esther's Notebooks* has been translated into eight languages. In 2016, Sattouf was named a Knight of France's Order of Arts and Letters.

www.riadsattouf.com